We Believe

We Believe

A Study of the Book of Confessions
for Church Officers

Revised Edition

Harry W. Eberts, Jr.

Westminster/John Knox Press
Louisville, Kentucky

Cover design by Drew Stevens

Published by Westminster/John Knox Press
Louisville, Kentucky

This book is printed on acid-free paper that meets the American National Standards Institute Z39.48 standard. ∞

PRINTED IN THE UNITED STATES OF AMERICA
9 8 7 6 5 4 3 2 1

Library of Congress Cataloging-in-Publication Data

Eberts, Harry W., 1926–
    We believe : a study of the Book of confessions for church officers / Harry W. Eberts, Jr. — Rev. ed.
        p.   cm.
    Includes bibliographical references.
    ISBN 0-664-25374-1 (alk. paper)
    1. Presbyterian Church U.S.A. Book of Confessions.
2. Presbyterian Church—Creeds—History. 3. Presbyterian Church—Church officers. I. Title.
    BX8969.5.E24   1993
    238'.5137—dc20   93-39392

Contents

Introduction

This study is intended to assist ordained officers of the Presbyterian Church (U.S.A.) to understand more fully what they say when they affirm the third ordination question:

> Do you sincerely receive and adopt the essential tenets of the Reformed faith as expressed in the confessions of our church as authentic and reliable expositions of what Scripture leads us to believe and do, and will you be instructed and led by those confessions as you lead the people of God? (*Book of Order*, G-14.0405c)

From 1729 into the late twentieth century, all three Presbyterian bodies that now make up the PCUSA used the Westminster documents as their sole confessional standards. During these years the ordination question related to the confessions was formulated like this:

> Do you sincerely receive and adopt the Confession of Faith and the Catechisms of this Church, as containing the system of doctrine taught in the Holy Scriptures?

Eventually questions arose concerning the adequacy of this formulation for a twentieth-century church. Could one centuries-old standard sum up the world of the Christian faith? What is meant by the phrase "system of doctrine"? In response, the Presbyterian Church in the United States adopted in 1962 "A Brief Statement of Belief" as a summary of its understanding of the Reformed faith. The United Presbyterian Church in the

United States of America took an even more far-reaching action, writing a new confession, the Confession of 1967, and making it part of a *Book of Confessions* that included eight other documents. In 1983, the year when The United Presbyterian Church in the United States of America and the Presbyterian Church in the United States merged to form the Presbyterian Church (U.S.A.), the General Assembly adopted a *Book of Confessions* with ten documents (the Westminster Larger Catechism, which had been omitted by the UPCUSA in 1967, was restored) and appointed a committee to write "A Brief Statement of the Reformed Faith," to be included in all future editions of the book. When quoting from creeds and confessions (except for A Brief Statement of Faith), we have used the texts and reference numbers found in the 1983 *Book of Confessions.* [1]

The eleven documents included in the *Book of Confessions* are drawn from various critical times in the life of the church.

Two come from the beginning of the Christian church, from what we now call the early catholic church. In the period from about A.D. 150 to 500 there were two centers of the Christian faith, Rome in the west and Constantinople in the east. The Apostles' Creed was developed for use in the western or Roman church, while the Nicene Creed grew out of the liturgy of the eastern or Orthodox churches.

More than a millennium later, the western churches underwent the revolution known as the Reformation. From the religious vitality unleashed by this religious cataclysm, unnumbered creeds, confessions, and catechisms were composed. Presbyterians now include three in the *Book of Confessions,* one each from Scotland, Germany, and Switzerland, countries where the Reformation was especially successful.

Three documents in the *Book of Confessions* have come from the post-Reformation church. These, a confession of faith and two catechisms, were written in England by the Westminster Assembly from 1643 to 1647 during the English civil war.

The other three, the Barmen Declaration, the Confession of

1967, and A Brief Statement of Faith, were written in the twentieth century, the first in Germany in the years leading up to World War II, the second by The United Presbyterian Church in the United States of America during the troubled 1960s, and the third by the newly merged Presbyterian Church (U.S.A.) as its first act of theological formation.

Before proceeding, we need to be clear about the meaning of the term "confession." The popular use as referring to an admission of sin and guilt is not the primary meaning when related to these documents. Rather, as stated in a report to the 198th General Assembly (1986) of the Presbyterian Church (U.S.A.): "To confess means openly to affirm, declare, acknowledge or take a stand for what one believes to be true."[2] While this kind of "confessing" frequently requires admitting one's guilt for stands previously taken or not taken (as we shall see in the Barmen Declaration), the basic emphasis is on affirmations made and not on sin committed.

Furthermore, the confessions found in the *Book of Confessions* are public rather than private statements. As the report noted, "The church writes confessions of faith when it faces a situation of life or a situation of death so urgent that it cannot remain silent but must speak, even at the cost of its own security, popularity, and success."[3] In short, the *Book of Confessions* contains public declarations made before God and the world of what—or, rather, in whom—the church believes.

Four different kinds of writings are included in the *Book of Confessions:* creeds, confessions, catechisms, and declarations. Creeds are short statements of belief, beginning with the Latin word *credo,* "I believe," or its equivalent; the Apostles' Creed and the Nicene Creed are examples. Confessions are more extensive statements of theological belief; the *Book of Confessions* includes the Scots Confession of 1560, the Second Helvetic Confession, the Westminster Confession of Faith, and the Confession of 1967. Catechisms are series of questions and answers about the faith; Presbyterians use the Heidelberg Catechism and the two Westminster catechisms, the Shorter and the Larger. The other confessional form is the declaration, a "here we stand, we can do no other" statement, made in the face of great evil; the Barmen Declaration is an example. The following chart lists these creeds and confessions, giving the name of the document, the authors (if known), the situation that occasioned its writing, and the theological viewpoint it represents. The main part of the book describes each confession in its historical context. The documents are grouped in four sections, as they are on the chart: the two creeds from the early church, the confessions and catechisms from the churches of the Reformation, those from the Westminster Assembly, and the three twentieth-century documents.

Creed or Confession	Date and Author	Occasion for Writing	Theological Position
Apostles' Creed	Between A.D. 160 and 180, in Rome; author unknown; added to frequently in the early catholic church; became the basic creed of the western church	The rise of Marcionism made the catholic church state its faith in this creed, which was used as a baptismal statement.	It states belief in God as Father, Son, Holy Spirit; describes work of each.
Nicene Creed	In 325 at the Council of Nicaea, and 381 at the Council of Constantinople; adopted by the bishops there; became the basic creed of the eastern church	The Emperor Constantine had just declared Christianity the official religion of the Roman empire and he requested that a statement of faith be drawn up. It was written in such a way as to combat the heresy of Arius and his followers who believed Jesus was simply a good man and not also Son of God.	Following and making more theologically accurate the trinitarian understanding of one God in three persons, it amplified the church's understanding of Christ (as of one substance with the Father) and described more completely the work of the Holy Spirit.

Creed or Confession	Date and Author	Occasion for Writing	Theological Position
Scots Confession	1560, by John Knox and others	When Scotland accepted the Reformed faith, Parliament asked the pastors to draw up a Confession of Faith, which they ratified on August 17, 1560. This was the basic confession of the Church of Scotland until 1688.	It covers the important items of reformation theology, and it breathes the spirit of churchmen who are prepared to be martyred for their faith. It affirms the infallibility of Scripture, and it is the most anti-popish of all our documents. It defines the church by (1) its pure preaching of the gospel, (2) right administration of the sacraments, and (3) the exercise of discipline, but it subordinates all to the rule and headship of Christ.

Creed or Confession	Date and Author	Occasion for Writing	Theological Position
Heidelberg Catechism	Heidelberg, Germany, 1563, by Zacharias Ursinus and Caspar Olevianus	Heidelberg had become a battleground between various understandings of the Reformation faith, and Frederick III, ruler of the Palatinate, asked that a catechism be written that would reconcile the contending parties.	Written in the first and second person, confessional style, this catechism sets forth our sin and misery, God's redemption for us in Christ, and our gratitude to God for the deliverance; it brings together repentance, faith, and love. It includes statements on the Apostles' Creed, the Lord's Prayer, the Ten Commandments, and the sacraments. Fresh, lively, and glowing, it is also dignified, brief, and truly eloquent.

Creed or Confession	Date and Author	Occasion for Writing	Theological Position
Second Helvetic Confession	Zurich, Switzerland, 1566, by Henry Bullinger	Originally composed by Bullinger, leader of the Reformation in Zurich, to state his own faith, it was redeveloped when Frederick III requested a statement of Reformed faith to present to the Lutherans who were trying to charge him with heresy.	It states that the Reform faith is in harmony with the true catholic faith of all ages. If the church has harmony with the essential doctrines of the ancient church, it can also have variety in the unessentials.
Westminster Confession and Larger and Shorter Catechisms	1645 to 1649, in London, England, at Westminster Abbey, by the Westminster Assembly of Divines	Parliament—recognizing that England was divided in both church and state between royalists, followers of parliament, and independents—called an Assembly to meet on July 1, 1643, to resolve the issues and bring order to church and state. Never adopted in England, it was through Scotland that this became the basic statement of faith for Presbyterian and Reformed churches.	The Westminster Confession sets out the doctrines of the church, and the catechisms are designed for the education of children and adult confirmands; they give the essence of the Christian faith. The documents are built upon the themes of the sovereignty of God and the duty humanity owes to this sovereign God.

Creed or Confession	Date and Author	Occasion for Writing	Theological Position
Barmen Declaration	May 29–31, 1934, in Barmen, Germany, written largely by Karl Barth	With the rise to power in Germany of Hitler and his attempt to control the church as he did all other institutions, the church split into a "German Christian party," built on folk, race, and blood, and a "Confessing Church" that tried to remain true to the teaching of the Christian church through the ages. This Confessing Church called a meeting in Barmen to set out its faith and counter the imminent Nazi takeover.	It declares that Jesus Christ alone is the one Word of God, the one source of all forgiveness, and that the church should never look to anyone or anything other than Christ as the source of its faith and life.

Creed or Confession	Date and Author	Occasion for Writing	Theological Position
The Confession of 1967	Adopted in 1967 by the General Assembly of the UPCUSA; about a decade went into its writing and its adoption by the church	In the tensions of the 1960s and the growing secularism of the nation, the church sought to bring up to date its statement of faith in a manner consistent with Scripture, the historic faith of the church, and the needs of the day.	Declaring that in Christ God offers reconciliation to the world, it sets the church on a ministry of reconciliation in a world wracked with tensions among classes, nations, and races, and within families.
A Brief Statement of Faith	Adopted in 1991 by the General Assembly of the Presbyterian Church (U.S.A.)	Upon the reunion in 1983 of the former United Presbyterian Church in the United States of America and the Presbyterian Church in the United States, the Plan for Reunion of the two General Assemblies authorized the writing of a statement that would summarize Reformed faith. Eight years in preparation, it was designed for use both in worship and in the classroom to bring theological identity and ecclesiastical integrity to the new church.	Based on 2 Corinthians 13:13 and drawing heavily upon Scripture and earlier confessions, A Brief Statement sets forth trinitarian doctrine in a confessional mode. Going beyond both the Apostles' and Nicene Creeds, it adds to the doctrine of Jesus Christ a statement concerning his life and ministry. It speaks of full equality of women and men in the church, including equality in the church's ordained offices. It also, for the first time, introduces concerns about ecological justice into a creed or confession.

1
Creeds of the Early Church

The Christian church that went out from Jerusalem into all Judea and Samaria and to the end of the earth (Acts 1:8) faced unbelievable questions and issues. It had to take a Jewish gospel into a Greek and Roman society. It had to proclaim a Lord who had been crucified by the Roman authorities and whom God had raised from the dead. It had to develop strategies for worship, education, administration, evangelism, and social action. It had to compete with religions whose practices were so ancient that they were lost in tradition and had to speak to philosophies that still make sense to some people. It had to bridge the vast distances of the Roman empire, traveling on foot, by donkey, and by boat. In the cities that were its destination, its churches contained little more than a handful of persons out of the million in Rome, the half million in Corinth, the third of a million in Alexandria, Antioch, and Ephesus. And it faced an empire and bureaucracy that was little more than tolerant when it was not downright hostile.

How did the church do it? Unfortunately, we cannot reconstruct the entire scenario. We do know, however, that the infant church out-thought, out-lived, and out-died its adversaries. This combination of clear theological thinking, strong ethical living, and determined martyrdom for the cause and its master, Jesus of Nazareth, became the basis on which the Christian church first survived and later thrived.

Some of this can be gathered from the two creeds in the *Book of Confessions* that are drawn from the early, catholic period of the church's life. Here can be seen the results of the church's thought as it developed its doctrines of the Trinity and the incarnation. On the Trinity: How could theologians explain the many ways God came to the church? The early theologians began by describing God as Father, Son, and Holy Spirit and working out in their own lives what that meant. On the incarnation: Who was this One who stood at the center of their faith? They soon found themselves saying that Jesus Christ was truly God and truly human, all that humankind could expect God to be and all that God expects every human person to be. Both of these doctrines are clearly stated in the two creeds.

What may not be immediately clear in the creeds is the understanding of the meaning and mission of the church that they contain. They understand the church to be the fellowship of the saints through which God in Christ offers forgiveness of sins. The church holds before its people and the whole world the promise of the resurrection of the body and of life everlasting. These identifying marks of the church are the basis of the message that Christianity carried into the dying world of Greek and Roman society. It promised a sense of belonging to those lost in the teeming, unfriendly cities of the Mediterranean world. It offered newness of life to people who thought the world was at its sunset, winding down like a dying day. It brought hope for life to come to those who were conditioned to have no hope.

These and other themes will be developed as we tell the story of the writing of the Apostles' and Nicene creeds.

The Apostles' Creed

The Apostles' Creed is the earliest, most rugged, and best known of the eleven documents that make up the creeds and confessions of the Presbyterian Church (U.S.A.). It was first formulated in Rome, sometime between the years A.D. 160 and 180. Within that twenty-year period a man named Marcion arrived in Rome with the intent of forcing the Christian church to accept the peculiar ideas he had worked out for himself and his followers, and which represented for many in the church an attack upon its faith.

Marcion was one of the colorful characters of the early Christian church. A native of Pontus in the region of the Black Sea in Asia Minor, a bishop's son, and a successful entrepreneur in merchandising, Marcion had begun to develop his own brand of Christianity and presented his peculiar views so openly that his own father excommunicated him from the church. Undaunted by this, he came to Rome and preached his position so powerfully that, as one of his opponents charged, he duped half the Christians in Rome into accepting his ideas.

His chief ideas grew out of his strong emotional responses to his own life situation. As a native of the bleak land around the Black Sea, he felt a sense of hostility toward the goodness of God's creation. As a son who had rebelled against his father, he could not accept God as father. As a successful businessman, he was suspicious of his competitors, many of whom, especially in his home city, were Jews or Jewish converts to Christianity. So he refused to call God the creator, for how, he asked, could a good God create mosquitoes, crocodiles, and vipers, and make the processes of begetting, birth, and death so vile? Borrowing a phrase from Plato, Marcion called God not creator but "Demi-urge," a lesser energy (that is the translation of the Greek word), a blundering craftsman who created a product of which nothing good can be said. He refused to call God "Father," either his father or the father of the Lord Jesus Christ, saying instead that Jesus himself was a spiritual being from a higher and unknown order who had come to earth to save us from the power of the Demiurge. He tried to erase from the Scriptures everything that was Jewish and said that the only Scripture any Christian needed to read consisted of ten of the letters of Paul (especially those that contrasted Christianity with Judaism) and an expurgated Gospel of Luke, the Gospel written by the traveling companion of his beloved Paul. Marcion and his disciples posed a sharp challenge to the Christian church, and the church in Rome responded in kind.

One of the responses of the Roman church (there were

other forms of response in addition to this one) was to develop
a creedal statement that refuted Marcion's position. In its first
form, the creed was quite brief, probably containing only the
following phrases:

> I believe in God, the all-sovereign Father.
> And in Jesus Christ his Son,
> The One born of Mary the Virgin,
> The One crucified under Pontius Pilate, and buried;
> the third day risen from the dead,
> ascended into the heavens,
> seated at the right hand of the Father,
> whence he will come to judge the living and the dead.
> And in Holy Spirit, resurrection of flesh.[4]

At the moment this was enough to rebut Marcion. The
statement emphasized the way God had been experienced by
the church: God was Father, the God and Father of Jesus
Christ. God was incarnate in the specific person of Jesus, who
was not only divine but also a human being born of Mary the
Virgin, crucified by the Roman governor Pontius Pilate, buried after death, then raised from the dead and who, according
to the faith of the church, ascended to the heavens as prime
minister of God's kingdom and was yet to come as judge of all.
And, as a miracle as great as any of the others, the church
affirmed that the spirit of Christ himself—the Holy Spirit of
God in Christ—continued with them in the trials and struggles
and joys of the Christian life.

The anti-Marcion nature of the creed is clear. Against Marcion's view of the creator as demiurge, the church affirmed the
creator as all-sovereign Father. Against the view that the God
of the New Testament was different from the God of the Old
Testament, the church declared that Jesus was God's Son.
Against the view that Jesus was never truly human, the church
emphasized his humanity as one who was born of woman and
who truly died a brutal death. Against the view that Jesus was
only the savior and never a judge, the church insisted that Jesus
would come to judge all. Against the view that flesh is evil and

life in the flesh is bad, the church claimed that this life is eternal. The doctrine of the "resurrection of flesh," that eternal life itself is a life of flesh, affirms the goodness of this life. The Christian leaders in Rome thus proceeded to refute, one by one, each of Marcion's doctrines.

But if the refutations provided the substance of the creed, the organization of the creed was drawn from another source. It took the form of the faith stated by Christians at the time of baptism: "I baptize thee in the name of the Father and of the Son and of the Holy Spirit."

This structure indicates the purpose for which the creed was originally intended, a statement of belief of persons who were to be baptized into the faith. In Rome, baptism was a dramatic occasion. Candidates for membership in the church had to undergo a lengthy period of instruction, rarely less than a year in duration, often as long as three. During this period candidates were given both moral and doctrinal instruction. The period of instruction intensified during Lent and in those sacred weeks was conducted by the bishop himself. On the night before Easter, those to be baptized were gathered in a baptistery and asked to state what they believed. In Rome after 180 they would say, "I believe in God, the all-sovereign Father," and repeat the creed in its earliest form. Just before dawn on Easter Day, the candidates were baptized by the bishop and then taken in procession to the church, where for the first time they joined with the whole congregation in celebrating the Lord's Supper.

Once the creed was formulated, it proved rugged and versatile, accepting numerous additions made to it in subsequent centuries in response to the changing needs of the church. Born in controversy, it survived and changed as the church faced and resolved the controversies of succeeding centuries.

A major difficulty for the church from 150 to 300 was persecution, which frequently took the form of requiring Christians to make sacrifices to the emperor at Rome. In practice this meant placing a bit of incense on the altar to the emperor (a contemporary equivalent would be a salute to the flag). Some

Christians did this, while others refused. Those who refused were often tortured and mutilated, and some were killed. But the persecutions did end, and the church continued to gather for worship, prayers, and the Supper. The question arose as to who should be admitted to these services: only those who had stood firm under persecution? Or should those who had fallen away also be welcomed? After much soul-searching, the church decided that those who had lapsed should be restored after they had publicly repented, and as a sign of reconciliation an additional phrase was added to the creed: "I believe in the forgiveness of sins."

Another controversy arose in the late fourth and early fifth centuries in North Africa when Augustine was bishop of Hippo. This revolved around the question of the manner in which the church could be called "universal." On one side stood a group called the Donatists, who held that any bishops who had knuckled under to Rome in the persecutions had forfeited their offices and could no longer be called "holy." Almost half the churches in North Africa held that position. On the other side stood Augustine, who insisted that the church consisted not only of the heroic Christians but of all sorts of Christians in all parts of the Roman world. Augustine's position prevailed, but not to the exclusion of the other, and to the words "holy church" was added the word "catholic," or universal, and the creed was now to state, "I believe in the holy [that is, morally firm] catholic [that is, universal] church."

Two other phrases were added to the creed in the fifth century. "He descended into hell" was added in Gaul, and the phrase apparently referred to the Lord of glory entering the region of darkness upon his death and bringing the light of life even there. "The communion of saints" was written into the creed about the same time and was designed to describe the constituency of the church; the "saint" is one who has been sanctified by the death and resurrection of Christ. The Christian church is indeed a community of those who have been set apart by the call of God in Christ to share fully in the life of faith.

In such a way through half a millennium, phrase by phrase, the Apostles' Creed was composed. It was not until the eighth century that the creed was completed in its present form. Even today the church determines the official form of the creed we use. In some congregations the phrase "the one holy universal Christian church" is used, substituting the word "universal" for "catholic," and in the Presbyterian *Hymnal* of 1933, in a footnote signaled by an asterisk at the phrase "he descended into hell," these words are interpreted to mean, "[he] continued in the state of the dead, and under the power of death, until the third day." The Apostles' Creed is the result of a gradual elaboration of a creed first stated in Rome between 160 and 180. With additions made to it in the following centuries, it came to be considered a fair and full statement of the faith delivered to the apostles and testified to in Scripture.

Without question it is the best known of all the creeds and confessions of the church, and the faith stated in it has worked itself most fully into the structures of belief of the Christian faith. It states our faith in the triune God, Father, Son, and Holy Spirit. God as Father is the creator and governor; God as Son is judge and redeemer; God as Holy Spirit continues to bring the blessings of the work of Jesus Christ to the Christian community.

The creed teaches about Christ by means of a series of verbs: was conceived, born, suffered, crucified, dead, buried, rose again, ascended, will come to judge. Some rather obvious omissions occur in the creed. It says nothing of Christ's role as teacher, healer, guide, or comforter, nor is it meant to replace any of the scriptural witnesses to Christ. It emphasizes the importance of the incarnation, atonement, and resurrection, but it does not develop any theology about these events. It tells us that we know Christ through what he does, the activities of his life, and it holds before us his birth, death, resurrection, and his coming again, and asks each of us to take these into account in our own Christian faith.

It also describes the work of the church. The Holy Spirit, as the spirit that animates the Christian community, continues to make available in ever-new forms the benefits bestowed through the life and death of Christ. From his ministry and through the church Christians receive the gift of fellowship with God and one another. The community of saints is the antidote to life's isolations and alienations; we receive the offering of forgiveness of sins—the resolution of our inadequacies and guilts. And we are offered the promise of the life to come, the resurrection of the body and the life eternal, God's answer to human fears of death and extinction.

The Apostles' Creed is a powerful statement of the Christian faith. But it did not prove to be a final statement. New issues arose in the church, and Christians were again called upon to discover more adequate ways to articulate the vitality of the message. One of these moments of decision arose in the fourth century in Asia Minor, and was to become the occasion for the formulation of the Nicene Creed.

The Nicene Creed

According to tradition, the Nicene Creed was formulated by the Council of Nicaea in A.D. 325 and was reaffirmed by the Council of Constantinople in 381. Tradition in this instance is not accurate, however, for the statement of faith called the Nicene Creed emerged, in its present form, from the church in Jerusalem sometime between those two dates.

Two major factors lay behind the formulation of a new creed at this point in the history of the church.

The first factor was the changed political situation in the Roman empire. The emperor Constantine had consolidated his hold over Rome by a series of brilliant victories in the western part of the empire, climaxed in 312 in the battle of the Milvian Bridge. Constantine, influenced by Christianity since his childhood and believing that his Christian faith had been decisive in his military victories, declared it to be the official religion of Rome. Since Christianity was unknown to many in the Roman empire, a statement of faith had to be composed in order to make it known to any and all.

The other factor was ecclesiastical. Increasingly divisive theological positions were occurring in the Christian church. Constantine's simple position of "one empire, one emperor, one God, one faith, one church" did not prove in practice to be acceptable to all. The emperor found to his dismay that the Christian church was dividing into two warring camps.

The split began, apparently, in a personal feud between two church leaders who knew each other well and disliked one another heartily. Alexander was bishop of Alexandria in Egypt, and Arius was one of the priests serving under him. Alexandria, long a center for Greek learning, had, through the work of such men as Clement and Origen, been transformed into the intellectual hub of the church. Its excellent catechetical school had trained priests and bishops from every part of the empire. Alexander, bishop of the diocese, was by no means a great theologian, although he was an excellent administrator. Arius fancied himself a more fitting heir than his bishop to the theological heritage of the city. This bright young priest began to deal with concepts and ideas about the relationship between God and Christ in a way that troubled the more stolid Alexander. Arius stated, "Our faith . . . is this: We know one God alone unbegotten, . . . who begot an only Son, . . . a perfect creature of God."[5] So the conflict was joined. Alexander and his followers insisted that the Son was co-equal and co-eternal with the Father, while the Arians submitted that the Son was a unique creation of the Father but, for all that, a creature of the Father's will.

After considerable sparring for position throughout the years 319 to 321, Alexander convened a synod in Egypt to address the issues. As a result of its debates, the synod deposed and excommunicated Arius and his followers. In exile, Arius went from Alexandria to Nicomedia in northern Asia Minor, the former capital city of the eastern branch of the Roman empire. The city, still the summer headquarters of the emperor, was presided over by a bishop favorable to Arius's position who was also a personal friend of the emperor. He drew Constantine into the ecclesiastical struggle, and the emperor called for a council to meet in the city of Nicaea in the summer of 325.

Nicaea today is a small and insignificant village in the hills a hundred miles south of Istanbul. In those days it was a thriving community in the eastern heartland of Rome's empire. About three hundred churchmen attended the council. Seventeen supported Arius and thirty sided with Alexander, the remainder being primarily interested in keeping the church's present peace, tranquillity, and position. Constantine, not yet a member of the church, also attended. Only two or three leaders from the western empire were able to be present, and Pope Sylvester himself was too old to make the long journey from Rome to Asia Minor. The opening day was spent in praising the emperor. It was clear that for the first time in three hundred years the church felt its position in the empire was secure.

After opening remarks from both sides, Eusebius of Caesarea presented a compromise position. He suggested that the Council adopt as its official statement a creed from Caesarea that was in use when he was baptized, and on which he was certain both sides could agree: "We believe in one God, all-governing Father, maker of all things, visible and invisible. And in one Lord Jesus Christ, . . . first-born of all creatures, who before all ages was begotten of the Father. . . . We believe also in one Holy Spirit."[6] This creed stated that the Father was the maker of all things, as the Arians suggested, and that Christ was the first-born of every creature (this made Christ one of God's created objects, as they also declared), but at the same time the Son was pre-existent with the Father, as Alexander proclaimed. It quickly appeared that both sides could agree on this creed.

The problem was that it was not agreement that Alexander desired. His aim was to exclude the Arians. So the compromise creed was sent to a committee for study. When it was reported out, it contained a phrase unacceptable to the Arians, *homoousia* (of the same substance), making the Son co-equal in all respects with the Father. It also contained anathemas: anyone who did not sign the new creed would be excommunicated. Arius and two followers would not sign it. Constantine then intervened in the proceedings by adding a new dimension to excommunication. Placing a political punishment atop the ecclesiastical one, he banished those who were excommunicated. Alexander had won the day, and Arius was banished.

The Arians made a quick comeback. One of their leaders, the bishop of Nicomedia, to whom Arius had fled from Alexandria early in the struggle and whose friendship with the emperor was instrumental in calling the council in the first place, interceded with Constantine. Arian supporters were quickly returned to positions of power within the church. By 357 the Arians felt they were strong enough to revoke the Nicene Creed. In response to their attack Athanasius, who had been bishop of Alexandria since Alexander's death and was now the chief defender of the Nicene statement, began to gather his forces. In wide-ranging skirmishes during the next twenty years, the Athanasians grew steadily stronger until, in the First Council of Constantinople in 381, the church reaffirmed the original Nicene Creed of 325 and deposed the remaining Arians.

It would be unfair, however, to see the victory of the Athanasians to be only the result of a power struggle in the church. Rather, the Nicene position won out because Athanasius' thinking about God prevailed in the church. Our salvation, said Athanasius, is from God, and if Christ be less than God, how can he bring about our salvation? God, in order to effect a fundamental change in human nature, came into human life in the person of Christ to accomplish this change. Humankind needs to be saved from the results of its own self-corruption, and this salvation comes through the incarnation of the Word of God. This needed salvation, proclaimed Athanasius, is what the Nicene Creed had been affirming all along.

When a document has been fought over as long and intensely as this original statement was, and when so many people have been wounded in the battles, it would seem wise to retire the battle-scarred document and turn to another. Precisely this occurred. The council at Constantinople in 381 turned to a creed that had been developed in Jerusalem during the bitter fifty years and which was already being used by many churches in the eastern empire. Influenced by the original Nicene document, to be sure, but going beyond it in a number of respects, the Jerusalem creed removed some of the offending phrases and described more fully the work of the Holy Spirit. As adopted by the council, it became known as the Constantinopolitan, Niceno-Constantinopolitan, or, commonly, the Nicene Creed. In a new translation,[7] it reads like this:

We believe in one God,
  the Father, the Almighty,
  maker of heaven and earth,
  of all that is, seen and unseen.

We believe in one Lord, Jesus Christ,
  the only Son of God,
  eternally begotten of the Father,
  God from God, Light from Light,
  true God from true God,
  begotten, not made,
  of one Being with the Father.
  Through him all things were made.
For us men and for our salvation
  he came down from heaven:
by the power of the Holy Spirit
  he became incarnate from the Virgin Mary, and was
  made man.
For our sake he was crucified under Pontius Pilate;
  he suffered death and was buried.
  On the third day he rose again
    in accordance with the Scriptures;
  he ascended into heaven
    and is seated at the right hand of the Father.

He will come again in glory to judge the living and
the dead,
    and his kingdom will have no end.

We believe in the Holy Spirit, the Lord, the giver of life,
·   who proceeds from the Father [and the Son].
With the Father and the Son he is worshiped and
glorified.
He has spoken through the Prophets.
We believe in one holy catholic and apostolic Church.
We acknowledge one baptism for the forgiveness of
sins.
We look for the resurrection of the dead,
    and the life of the world to come. Amen.

This creed set the boundaries for later discussion in the
church: the full God, who as the Father had created all things,
had to be fully at work in Christ to offer salvation. This God
continues to offer salvation through the work of the Holy
Spirit in the life of the church.

Just how these theological insights can best be understood
has engaged the minds of Christians in all the generations, and
no single essay can even begin to indicate the richness of the
interpretation that has been offered concerning this creed.
Perhaps the most promising line of interpretation was proposed very early, around the year 350 by three men from
Cappadocia: Basil of Caesarea, Gregory of Nazianzus, and
Gregory of Nyssa. They used the word *prosōpon* (Latin *persona*)
to describe the mysterious activity by which God is revealed
in human life. This word was a term drawn from Greek drama,
where it denoted the mask that actors wore to portray the
various characters of the drama. On the Greek stage one actor
usually played more than one role, and the role being played
at the moment was identified by the mask, the persona, being
worn. So they suggested that, according to this analogy, the
one God takes on three characterizations in interacting in the
human drama: as Father, the one God creates all things; as Son,

the one God redeems; as Holy Spirit, the one God continues
to make the benefits of creation and redemption available.
through the church to God's people. God plays three roles; but
no matter in which role we see God, it is the one God fully
engaged with God's people in playing out God's part in the
human drama.

Perhaps the greatest interpreter of the Nicene Creed was
not a theologian at all but a church musician of deep piety and
Christian understanding. Johann Sebastian Bach incorporated
the creed into his magnificent Mass in B Minor. In it Bach
focused on what God did in Christ as being the central act in
human life. The composer pictured God enthroned amid the
trumpets of heaven. He declared the mystery of the incarnation in music of extraordinary grace and sensitivity. When he
came to the scene of Calvary, Bach simply repeated again and
again the word *crucifixus* ("crucified"). In this scene all humanity stands in amazed horror before the uplifted cross and its
tortured victim, while in the last five bars the hushed saddened
voices seem to lower the sufferer into his tomb. Then, on
Easter Day, we are dazzled as composer and musicians glorify
the One who rises from the dead. Bach is correct: the center
of the creed is Jesus Christ, his incarnation, death, and resurrection. A creed is more than a precise formulation of belief. It
is in addition a chorus of praise to the God who creates us and
redeems us, and whose presence never leaves us.

2
The Reformation Church

The Reformation of the Christian church may be said to have begun in the experience of one man, Martin Luther, monk, priest, and professor at the University of Wittenberg.

Luther was an intellectual in search of personal salvation. He tried every means of assurance that the Catholic Church of his day had to offer distraught souls. He became a monk and a good one. He confessed his sins, endlessly as it seemed to his confessors, until he wore out both them and himself. He made a pilgrimage to the holy city of Rome to pray before the blessed relics there. He became a priest. Finally he turned to the study of the Bible.

There he found the satisfaction for his soul that he could not find elsewhere in all the immense apparatus that the church had to offer. As God spoke to him through the Book, he came to know forgiveness for his sins, and release from the terrors that had enslaved him, as a man of the Middle Ages. Luther began to tell others of the good news he had received, and what he experienced proved to be the experience of many others. They responded to Luther's writing and preaching and the Reformation began, in the year 1517.

There were conditions beyond the experience of one man that contributed to the Reformation, of course. New frontiers of learning were being opened up as scholars peered into the treasures of the past and scientists probed the edges of the future. A New World had been discovered; just twenty-five years separated Luther from Christopher Columbus, and it took at least that long for the impact of the new discoveries to make its way into the minds and hearts of people. New wealth came from the new discoveries, and a whole new class of people, the bourgeoisie—the middle class of merchants and entrepreneurs—began to replace in influence and position the landed classes of the Middle Ages. Even the peasants began to ask for a place in the sun, and their movement was one that Luther and many of his followers could never understand.

Whole cities soon began to be taken over by the Reformation movement. The process was not as difficult as it seemed. A few men, following Luther's ideas, would move in on the established churches, run out the priests who had been placed there—not too hard a task, because many of them were too ignorant to know what was going on and too corrupt to care much anyway—change the worship to fit what came to be called the "Protestant" style, and then attempt to teach the people of the city the Protestant ways. This Luther did in Wittenberg, Zwingli in Zurich, Bucer in Strasburg, and Calvin in Geneva.

As the Roman Catholic Church fought back the struggle became increasingly bitter. Some lands and territories, like Italy, France, and Spain, remained Catholic. Some became Lutheran, as did much of Germany and the Scandinavian countries. Some, like England, went their own way. Some, namely, Switzerland, Holland, Scotland, Hungary, and Czech lands, followed the tenets of what became known as the Reformed faith set forth by John Calvin. So the Reformation in one way or another affected all Europe and all the lands touched by Europeans.

Theological issues were plentiful, including the old ones of the nature of God and God's relation to Christ. New issues arose concerning the authority of Scripture, the understanding of the sacraments, the nature of the ministry, the relationship between church and state. All these found their way into the innumerable creeds, confessions, and catechisms that were composed at this time.

All the great persons of the Reformation took part in this

process. Luther wrote catechisms and participated in the composition of confessions. A generation later Calvin and his compatriots did the same. The writings that have made their way into the *Book of Confessions,* however, come from the next generation of Reformers, those who, while often born Catholic, had early transferred or been transferred by their parents' preference into the Protestant faith and had been educated at the universities under Protestant professors. It is to these writings that we turn now, to see what they have to tell us of the meaning of the Reformed faith.

The Scots Confession

When John Knox and his friends concluded the Confession of Faith that they had prepared for the newly liberated Scottish Kirk, they did so with a prayer. The prayer was appropriate to the situation; the church of Scotland was at the point of winning freedom from its long oppression by the Roman Church, and the prayer called upon God to act in behalf of the church to scatter its enemies and to strengthen its resolve:

Arise, O Lord, and let thine enemies be confounded; let them flee from thy presence that hate thy godly Name. Give thy servants strength to speak thy Word with boldness, and let all nations cleave to the true knowledge of thee. Amen. (3.251)

The confession was written in Scotland in the turbulent year of 1560. Scotland was trying to preserve its national sovereignty from French incursions made in an effort to bring Scotland under the French rule in order to use it as a military base from which to attack England. John Knox, who had returned to Scotland from Geneva, Switzerland, just a year before, rallied the Protestant nobles to withstand the French endeavors. On June 11, 1560, the Queen Regent of France, Mary of Guise, who had set the plot in motion, died in her sleep, and within a month, on July 6, the Treaty of Edinburgh for the mutual protection of England and Scotland, was signed.

Because of this active alliance, France could no longer dominate Scotland, and by the treaty England voluntarily declared that she would no longer attempt to do so. Scotland was a free nation.

It also became a Protestant nation. On August 1, 1560, the Scottish Parliament convened at Edinburgh. It asked the Protestant ministers to draw up a Confession of Faith. Six men named John—Knox, Winram, Spottiswood, Willock, Douglas, and Row—were assigned the task. Four days later, on August 17, 1560, the document was reported to and ratified by the Parliament as "doctrine grounded upon the infallible Word of God." Scotland had her new nation, her new religion, and her new statement of faith.

The struggle to accomplish this had been severe. In the previous centuries the church of Scotland had become incredibly corrupt. The monasteries and the cathedrals had become enormously wealthy, owning half the land and controlling the parliament. Many parishes lacked priests, and those that had priests often found them uneducated and immoral men. But the times were changing, and the medieval life-style was crumbling before the revolutionary atmosphere of the sixteenth century. Scotland began to be affected by the work of Martin Luther. Men began to die for the new faith: Patrick Hamilton, a young nobleman, was burned at the stake in 1528, and George Wishart, a Protestant preacher, followed his path in 1546. The blood of martyrs nurtured the seed of the church, and in December 1557, Protestant nobles signed a covenant in Edinburgh to defend to the death "the whole Congregation of Christ and every member thereof." In 1559, John Knox— who had been captured in battle by the French fleet off St. Andrews in 1547 and made a galley slave for nineteen months, had escaped from slavery, and had gone to Geneva to study with John Calvin—returned to Scotland to renew the Protestant claims on the nation. In 1560, the Scottish Kirk became the established church of the nation, and the new Confession of Faith became its statement of belief. In 1572, the General Assembly of the Kirk also accepted the Second Helvetic Confession, Calvin's catechism, and the Heidelberg Catechism as approved statements of faith alongside the Scots Confession.

Two things stand out in the Scots Confession. It was written with the Apostles' Creed in mind, and it was written with a preacher's pen. It was not so much a statement of belief as it was a call to commitment; it was of the heart more than of the mind; it contained not the logician's propositions but the proclaimed word of the pulpit. Its preacher writers had stood before their congregations to preach the faith that had produced the Reformation in Scotland, and when they sat down in committee it was in the language of preaching that they expressed their thoughts. The Scots Confession of 1560 is a lengthy hortatory sermon with a prayer at the end.

Its structure, following that of the Apostles' Creed, consisted of five parts. The sermon began with an expression of faith in God—Father, Son, and Holy Spirit. It examined the place of the kirk in God's providence, and it discussed the Scriptures and sacraments upon which the kirk is built. (The Scottish preachers used the word "kirk" for the people of God instead of "church." Like "church," the word "kirk" is based on the Greek word *kyriakon*, "belonging to the Lord," but is closer to the Greek in spelling and sound. Since the Reformed movement in Scotland looked upon its task as that of obedience to the lordship of Jesus Christ, and wished to emphasize it, this word fit their militant mood.) It closed with a vision of the consummation that God was about to bring to believers in God's own good time.

"We confess and acknowledge one God alone," they began, "to whom alone we must cleave, whom alone we must serve, whom only we must worship, and in whom alone we put our trust." The verbs used—cleave, serve, worship, trust, each a verb of commitment—constitute a call to the kirk to be faithful to God. Only then do the writers go on to talk of the God to whom this faith is committed: the God who creates, rules, and guides all things in heaven and on earth by the inscrutable providence that manifests God's glory.

In the fullness of time God sent forth the Son, true man and true God. "That same eternal God and Father, who by grace alone chose us in his Son Christ Jesus before the foundation of the world was laid, appointed him to be our head, our brother, our pastor, and the great bishop of our souls." Jesus Christ, who offered himself in voluntary sacrifice, remained the only and well-beloved Son of his Father and is our only sacrifice for sin. Unable to be held in the sorrows of death, he rose for our justification in the same body in which he was crucified and buried, and he ascended into heaven. From there he shall come to bring judgment to his enemies and refreshment and restitution to those who have suffered violence and wrong for righteousness' sake, who shall inherit the blessedness promised them from the beginning.

With the ascension of Christ came the promised spirit, the Holy Ghost, who brings us into all truth. From the Spirit comes the kirk; it is "catholic, that is, universal, because it contains the chosen of all ages, of all realms, nations, and tongues," and it is "invisible, known only to God who alone knows whom he has chosen." There follows the most famous statement of the confession, the definition of the kirk worked out in Scotland but drawn from the experience of Reformed churches all over Europe:

> The notes of the true Kirk [are these]: first, the true preaching of the Word of God, in which God has revealed himself to us; . . . secondly, the right administration of the sacraments of Christ Jesus, with which must be associated the Word and promise of God to seal and confirm them in our hearts; and lastly, ecclesiastical discipline uprightly ministered, as God's word prescribes, whereby vice is repressed and virtue nourished. Then wherever these notes are seen and continue for any time . . . there, beyond any doubt, is the true Kirk of Christ, who, according to his promise, is in its midst. (3.18)

This kirk, unlike the earlier church of Scotland, is based not on the authority of the pope but upon the Scriptures of the Old and New Testaments. Scripture, asserts the confession, expresses "all things necessary to be believed for the salvation of man" (3.18). Since the Bible is a complex book, what interpretation of Scripture is authoritative? This answer is suggested: "The interpretation of Scripture, we confess, does not belong to any private or public person, nor yet to any Kirk, . . . but pertains to the Spirit of God by whom the Scriptures were written" (3.18). But if no private person in the quiet of one's heart, nor a public person in pulpit or assembly, has authority to interpret Scripture, how is it to be done? The confession offers this further refinement: "What the Holy Ghost uniformly speaks within the body of the Scriptures are what Christ Jesus himself did and commanded," these are the authoritative words in this authoritative book. "We dare not," they said in conclusion, "receive or admit any interpretation which is contrary to any principal point of our faith, or to any other plain text of Scripture, or to the rule of love" (3.18). Their description is significant for the church today as it struggles with the question of the authority of the Bible: authoritative Scripture, says this confession, is what Christ did and commands; it consists of the principal points of the Protestant faith; it is the plain text of Scripture; it is the rule of love.

The sacraments, Baptism and the Lord's Supper, also play a significant part in the life of the kirk, "not only to make a visible distinction between his people and those who were without the Covenant, but also to exercise the faith of his children and . . . seal in their hearts the assurance of his promise, and of that most blessed conjunction, union, and society, which the chosen have with their Head, Christ Jesus" (3.21). In the Supper, "true faith carries us above all things that are visible, carnal, and earthly, and makes us feed upon the body and blood of Christ Jesus. . . . He remains in [us] and [we] in him; [we] are so made of flesh of his flesh and bone of his bone that as the eternal Godhood has given to the flesh of Christ Jesus . . . life and immortality, . . . so the eating and drinking of the flesh and blood of Christ Jesus does the [same] for us" (3.21).

The final chapter of the confession points to the consumma-

tion under God of all things. Those who "believe with the
heart and boldly confess the Lord Jesus with their mouths shall
certainly receive his gifts. . . . In this life they shall receive
remission of sins, . . . [and] in the general judgment, there shall
be given to every man and woman resurrection of the flesh"
(3.25). The confession climaxes in a doxology:

> Such as continue in well doing until the end, boldly con-
> fessing the Lord Jesus, shall receive glory, honor, and
> immortality, we constantly believe, to reign forever in life
> everlasting with Christ Jesus, to whose glorified body all
> his chosen shall be made like, when he shall appear again
> in judgment and shall render up the Kingdom to God his
> Father. . . . To whom, with the Son and the Holy Ghost,
> be all honor and glory, now and ever. Amen. (3.251)

With these words the sermon reaches its peroration, and it
now proceeds to its prayer.

The Heidelberg Catechism

Legend has it that the occasion for the writing of the Heidelberg Catechism was a fist fight between Lutherans and Cal-
vinists that took place near the altar of the Church of the Holy
Spirit in Heidelberg, Germany, on Easter Day, 1562. Whether
or not the legend is totally accurate, there is sufficient substance
behind it to account for the composition of this significant
statement of faith.

Heidelberg was a university town on the western border of
the Germanic countries. A few miles from where the Neckar
River joins the Rhine, the historic dividing line between Germany and France, the Neckar Valley widens just enough to
permit the presence of a town. This is Heidelberg, pic-
turesquely located beside the river and between the hills on
both sides, its castle on the southern ridge guarding the valley,
the spires of its churches rising above the houses of the city and
the halls of the university. The university had been established
in 1346, and the town itself had become the seat of govern-

ment of the Palatinate region of Germany. With government and university in the same location, the town became a center for controversy as the Reformation developed.

Luther himself had come to lecture in Heidelberg in 1518, hardly a year after the Reformation began, and his presentation was so persuasive that a young Dominican monk named Martin Bucer left the monastery to become a Protestant. This same Bucer later became the protector and teacher of John Calvin when Calvin sought refuge in Bucer's church in Strasburg after having been exiled from Geneva in 1538. The town and area of Heidelberg became Lutheran in 1546, the year of Luther's death, when the Elector of the Palatinate, the ruler of the region, decreed that its worship and polity would henceforth follow Lutheran patterns. Philip Melanchthon, Luther's fellow reformer and gentle soul mate, was a graduate of the university at Heidelberg, and while he left his hometown to join Luther on the faculty of the university in Wittenberg, he remained the spiritual father of the town. But Heidelberg itself soon became a battleground of contending faiths. Catholic France was nearby, and was aggressive in protecting the faith of the Roman Church. Calvinist theologians and preachers came north along the Rhine from Switzerland to persuade church people of the rightness of their views. Lutherans, worried about both, dug in their heels and determined that the town would remain firmly within the Lutheran camp. The Peace of Augsburg, signed in 1555, a treaty between Catholics and Lutherans, exacerbated the predicament by forbidding the introduction of Calvinist teachings into German lands and cities. Clearly the situation was ripe for confrontation.

The face-off came when the leading Lutheran, Tilemann Hesshus, a professor of theology at the university and leader of the Lutheran clergy of Heidelberg, introduced a rigorist Lutheran position on the practice of the Lord's Supper into the worship of the church. He excommunicated those who did not hold his view. This controversy extended to a dispute at the altar over possession of the communion cup, who should hold it, who should give it, what should be said at the service of the

Supper. At that moment Frederick III, the newly installed Elector of the Palatinate, decided that the struggle had gone far enough and that he should take a direct hand in resolving it.

Frederick had come to his office in 1559, just as the dispute was growing in intensity. The office of Elector was a noble one, its holder was one of seven governors of Germanic provinces who had the right to elect the Holy Roman emperor. Frederick was not only powerful, he was a man of deep personal piety, of simple life-style (he lived simply so that he might contribute liberally from his private income to the cause of learning and religion), and of considerable intellectual acumen. He had made a personal study of the theological issues that were dividing his people. He had consulted with Melanchthon just before the latter's death in 1560 as to ways to deal with the struggle. Now he took two decisive actions: he banished Hesshus and his antagonists from the city, and he asked two young men of Heidelberg, Zacharias Ursinus and Caspar Olevianus, to prepare a catechism upon which all sides could agree.

The two men proved to be excellent choices for the task at hand. Zacharias Bär (Ursinus is the Latinized form of his name) had spent seven years at Wittenberg studying with Melanchthon and had come to Heidelberg to teach in the fall of 1561. Twenty-seven years old, he had also studied briefly with Calvin in Geneva and for a longer time with Peter Martyr in Zurich. He was fully conversant with the whole field of theology, and at the same time was at home in the classics and in poetry. His co-worker, Caspar Olewig (in Latin it became Olevianus), had studied in the same law colleges as had John Calvin, Orleans and Bourges, had studied for a year with Calvin in Geneva, and, though only twenty-four at the time, had been brought to Heidelberg by Frederick in January 1560 as professor at the university and preacher to the city. These two men, with Frederick in active support, worked over an earlier catechism that Ursinus had written, using its outline and some ninety of its questions and answers, and in September 1562 they had their new catechism in hand. In January 1563 it was published and given to the world.

The outline of the catechism is set out in Question Two: "How many things must you know that you may live and die in the blessedness of [Christian] comfort?" Answer: "Three. First, the greatness of my sin and wretchedness. Second, how I am freed from all my sins and their wretched consequences. Third, what gratitude I owe to God for such redemption" (4.002). This question and its answer illustrate some of the catechism's important points:

1. It is a catechism rather than a creed or confession. This means that it is cast in question-and-answer form rather than as a statement of belief, as are the Apostles' and Nicene creeds, or a declaration of faith and commitment, as is the Scots Confession. There is firm belief and solid commitment in it, of course, but since it is a catechism, this belief and commitment are set out in dialogic form.

2. The catechism is personal. It is stated in the first and second person rather than in the third; the questioner puts a question to "you," and the answer begins with "I." The spiritual and religious concerns of the whole person are addressed, not the concerns of the mind alone, and the answers given involve the total life and faith of the person responding.

3. The catechism is biblical. Its outline follows that of Paul's Letter to the Romans, which deals with the same three major themes. Moreover, wherever possible in the answers to the questions, it uses biblical language. It represents the Christian who is trying to live out his or her faith on the basis of the Word of God in Scripture and in Jesus Christ.

4. The catechism is irenic. Only one question, number 80, is in any way polemic. It deals with the difference between the papal Mass and the Protestant's Lord's Supper, and was not in the catechism as it was originally published. It was inserted only after the Roman Catholic Council of Trent, on

September 17, 1562, had reaffirmed transubstantiation as the sole official interpretation of the Lord's Supper and had anathematized anyone who disagreed. In no other way does this catechism reflect the struggles that called it forth but transcends them in a spirit of peace like that of Jesus Christ himself.

5. The catechism is ecumenical. It was written to provide a basis for restoring Reformed and Lutheran Christians to fellowship with each other. Its writers were educated in the widest possible Reformation traditions, and they had personal knowledge of the theologies of Luther, Melanchthon, Zwingli, and Calvin. After the catechism was published, it was used in churches in Germany, Holland, Hungary, Scotland, and later the United States. Its theology is catholic, that is, universal in appeal; reformed, expressing the faith of reformation times; and evangelical, setting forth the gospel message of Jesus Christ.

6. The catechism is a tool for preaching. Very early its 129 questions were organized into 52 sections so that one section might be used for preaching on each Lord's Day. This pattern is followed in our *Book of Confessions.* Congregations nourished on this kind of preaching, usually done in afternoon or evening services, were bound to be fully informed of the meaning of their faith and spiritually nurtured to put it into practice in their lives.

7. The catechism is a tool for teaching. Like other catechisms of the time, it focuses upon the Ten Commandments, the Apostles' Creed, the Lord's Prayer, and the sacraments of Baptism and the Lord's Supper. By doing so it indicates that if the Christian knows these and internalizes their meanings, that in itself is the best way to produce the kind of saving faith the Reformation teachers were trying to instill in the minds, hearts, and wills of the people of the church.

8. The catechism is a theological statement, and how it places creed, commandments, and Lord's Prayer within the framework of the document is important to the theological understanding of the work.

Jesus' summary of the law, for example, is placed at the beginning of the catechism. "Where do you learn of your sin and its wretched consequences?" we are asked in Question 3, and in answer we are told that we do so "From the Law of God." But the law to which we are pointed is not the Ten Commandments. It is Jesus' summary of the law, "You shall love the Lord your God with all your heart, and with all your soul, and with all your mind. . . . You shall love your neighbor as yourself." It is by looking to Jesus Christ, in other words, not to the law of the Old Testament, that we know our sin and misery, and how evil, perverse, corrupt, and perverted we are. But looking to Christ also brings us to salvation, and so the catechism points us to Christ and not to the law of the Old Testament, because Christ can save us and the law of the Old Testament cannot. Christ is our judge, but he is also our savior.

What then of the law of the Old Testament? The writers of this catechism place it, along with prayer, in the last section of their work, which deals with gratitude. Through prayer and the good works done by keeping the law, the Christian expresses thankfulness to God for the redemption granted in Christ. Prayer, says Answer 116, "is the chief part of the gratitude which God requires of us, and because God will give his grace and Holy Spirit only to those who sincerely beseech him in prayer without ceasing, and who thank him for these gifts" (4.116). Good works fit into the same category. Good works, says Answer 91, are "only those which are done out of true faith, in accordance with the Law of God, and for his glory, and not those based on our own opinion or on the traditions of men" (4.091). This is fully in accord with John Calvin's famous "third use of the law." Whereas Luther had provided only two uses for the law—the law as convicting us of and punishing us for our sins—Calvin had discovered that keeping the commandments is a positive way of showing our gratitude to God. In placing its discussion of the law at the end of the work, the Heidelberg Catechism exhibits its Calvinist parentage.

It does so also in its emphasis upon the importance of

redemption, and this can be seen in the number of questions allotted to each of its themes. Nine questions only deal with human sin and guilt. Forty-four questions are required to set out the thankfulness we owe God. Seventy-four questions are devoted to our redemption.

"Who is this mediator who is at the same time true God and a true and perfectly righteous man?" asks Question 18. Answer: "Our Lord Jesus Christ, who is freely given to us for complete redemption and righteousness" (4.018). Who then is saved? asks Question 20. "Only those who, by true faith, are incorporated into him and accept all his benefits" (4.020). Question 21 asks: "What is true faith?" The answer: "It is not only a certain knowledge by which I accept as true all that God has revealed to me in his Word, but also a wholehearted trust which the Holy Spirit creates in me through the gospel, that, not only to others, but to me also God has given the forgiveness of sins, everlasting righteousness and salvation, out of sheer grace solely for the sake of Christ's saving work" (4.021).

Certain knowledge and wholehearted trust in God's grace in the gift of Christ; that is the key to the Christian life. The catechism points to this grace by describing the Apostles' Creed and by holding the sacraments of Baptism and the Lord's Supper before us as the means by which we place ourselves under the power of the saving grace of God in Christ.

God the Father is not presented in a speculative but in a trusting way, as in the answer to Question 26: "The eternal Father of our Lord Jesus Christ, who out of nothing created heaven and earth with all that is in them, who also upholds and governs them by his eternal counsel and providence, is for the sake of Christ his Son my God and my Father. I trust in him so completely that I have no doubt that he will provide me with all things necessary for body and soul" (4.026).

God the Son is presented by discussing those portions of the Apostles' Creed that deal with the work of God through Jesus Christ. Christ is Savior, the Anointed One, the Only-begotten Son, our Lord. When asked, in Question 32, "Why are you called a Christian?" I reply, "Because through faith I share in Christ and thus in his anointing, so that I may confess his name, offer myself a living sacrifice of gratitude to him, and fight against sin and the devil with a free and good conscience throughout this life and hereafter rule with him in eternity over all creatures" (4.032).

God the Holy Spirit is seen as including us in the communion of saints, offering us the forgiveness of sins, and holding before us the comfort of the resurrection of the body and the life everlasting.

That we have faith in Christ is seen in our response to the preaching of the gospel and the use of the holy sacraments. Baptism, says Answer 69, by its sign of external washing is an assurance that the sacrifice of Christ on the cross avails to those who have true faith in him. Participating in the Lord's Supper, says Answer 76, "is not only to embrace with a trusting heart the whole passion and death of Christ, and by it to receive the forgiveness of sins and eternal life. In addition, it is to be so united more and more to his blessed body by the Holy Spirit dwelling both in Christ and in us that, although he is in heaven and we are on earth, we are nevertheless flesh of his flesh and bone of his bone, always living and being governed by one Spirit, as the members of our bodies are governed by one soul" (4.076).

"Wretched man that I am!" wrote Paul in the seventh chapter of Romans. "Who will save me from this body of death? Thanks be to God through Jesus Christ our Lord." This is the spirit of the Heidelberg Catechism as it speaks of our sin and misery, the redemption God has brought to us in Jesus Christ, and our gratitude for this redemption. Nowhere is this captured better than in the first question of the catechism: "What is your only comfort, in life and in death?" In answer we say:

That I am not my own,
but I belong
    body and soul,

in life and in death,
to my faithful Savior Jesus Christ.

He has fully paid for all my sins with his precious blood,
   and has set me free from the tyranny of evil.
He also watches over me in such a way
   that not a hair can fall from my head
   without the will of my Father in heaven:
in fact, all things must work together for my salvation.

Because I belong to him,
Christ, by his Holy Spirit,
assures me of eternal life
and makes me wholeheartedly willing and ready
   from now on to live for him.[8]

The Second Helvetic Confession

Frederick III, the elector of the Palatinate, survived the crisis
that created the Heidelberg Catechism only to be thrust into
a second critical theological struggle. This disagreement resulted in the preparation for public use of the document known
as the Second Helvetic Confession. Frederick, a gracious and
pious ruler, had joined the Reformed church after the publication of the Heidelberg Catechism, and shortly thereafter, in
1565, the Lutherans of his area charged him with heresy and
apostasy. In need of some defense against the charges, Frederick wrote to Heinrich Bullinger, a pastor in Zurich, who since
the death of John Calvin in 1564 had been the acknowledged
leader of the Reformed movement. Bullinger sent Frederick
a copy of a confession of faith that he had written for his own
use some time before. Frederick was so pleased with it that he
asked if it could be published in Latin and German and used
before the Imperial Diet (the ruling body of Germany) when
it assembled for his trial at Augsburg in 1566. Using the document as the basis for his own confession of faith, Frederick was
fully exonerated when the Diet met, and the proceedings for
his impeachment were dropped.

In the meantime, the churches in Switzerland recognized a need for a confession of faith that would create a closer bond of union among them. They discarded former confessions they had written: the so-called First Helvetic Confession, which had been prepared in Basel in 1536 and of which Heinrich Bullinger had been one of the authors; the Zurich Consensus of 1549; and the Geneva Consensus of 1552. The latter two had appeared in times of controversy and had dealt only with vexing questions related to the Lord's Supper and predestination. Bullinger's confession, which he had sent to Frederick, became the basis for current discussions. Theodore Beza, Calvin's successor in Geneva, suggested a few changes. These Bullinger gladly accepted, and the document was completed. It was approved by all the leading churches of Switzerland except Basel, which had its own confession and felt no need for another. It was published in Zurich on March 12, 1566, in Latin and German, and was translated into French by Beza later that summer.

Except for the Heidelberg Catechism, the Second Helvetic Confession became the most widely adopted confession of the European Reformed churches. It spread from the churches in Switzerland to Hungary (1567), France (1571), and Poland (1571). It was used in the Netherlands, England, and Scotland, and was translated into English, Dutch, Hungarian, Polish, Italian, Arabic, and Turkish. The testament of faith sent in a personal letter to the elector Frederick had become a statement employed in public confession by Christians over all of Europe and the Middle East.

Heinrich (Henry) Bullinger, its author, was born July 18, 1504, in Bremgarten in the Aargau district of Switzerland. He was the youngest of five sons of the Roman Catholic priest of that city. (This means, of course, that Heinrich was an illegitimate son, for his father, like many priests of that day, lived in an illegitimate yet tolerated marriage.) Educated in the school of the Brethren of the Common Life at Emmerich and at the University of Cologne, he was led by the writings of Luther and Melanchthon to study the Bible. He became a Protestant, and was called to succeed his father, now also a Protestant, in the pastorate of his home church in Bremgarten. When Ulrich Zwingli, the first Protestant reformer in Switzerland, was killed in the battle of Cappel in 1531, Bullinger was called on December 23, 1531, to be Zwingli's successor in the church in Zurich. He filled that post ably until his death in 1575. He was a model Reformed minister, and because of that his ministry is worth careful study.

Bullinger was an indefatigable preacher. From 1531 to 1542 he preached six or seven times a week; after that he limited his preaching to Sundays and Fridays. He followed the practice of Zwingli in explaining whole books of Scripture from the pulpit.

He was a devoted pastor who kept his home open from morning until night to visitors and those in need. He was especially generous with exiles and orphans, secured a decent pension for the widow of Ulrich Zwingli, and educated two of Zwingli's children with his own. He even visited people who were suffering from the plague to bring them the consolations of Christ, a most difficult task for a pastor of those days to do because it meant subjecting his own life to the risk of the dread disease; many pastors quailed before this terrifying task.

He was active in education and as pastor of the church was also the superintendent of the schools of Zurich. He saw to it that the University of Zurich was well supplied with able theologians.

A writer of broad theological interests, he wrote commentaries, in Latin, on all the books of the New Testament except Revelation. (John Calvin, curiously enough, had done the same.) He published sermons drawn from the Old Testament prophets, the Ten Commandments, the Apostles' Creed, and the sacraments. He wrote a history of the Swiss Reformation.

Like other Reformation pastors, Bullinger kept up a wide correspondence with other reformers throughout Europe. He was especially active in relating to the Reformation in England and was a friend and spiritual adviser to many of the English

Protestants. His death was lamented in England as a public calamity.

Unlike some of the reformers, he was tolerant of dissent and gentle in the treatment of his opponents. When Lutheran pastors were driven from Swabia in 1548 he received them in Zurich and treated them hospitably, even those who from their pulpits had denounced Reformed doctrine. He opposed the Anabaptists in his writings, but he never consented to their persecution. He had to remove one of his theological professors, who was also his best friend, from his office for what he considered heretical views, but he continued the man's salary until the day of his death. He wrote into his confession the gentle moderation he practiced in his life.

Heinrich Bullinger was also a model family man. He had married in 1529—his wife, like Luther's, was a former nun—and loved to play with his children and grandchildren and write them verses at Christmas. Like many overworked Protestant pastors of the time, his last years were sad ones. The plague of 1564–65 brought him near death and took his wife, three daughters, and a brother-in-law. His youngest daughter took care of his health. He preached his last sermon on Pentecost 1575, gathered his friends to him in August to take leave of them, and died on September 17, after having recited some of the psalms and the Lord's Prayer in the presence of his remaining family.

Bullinger wrote the first edition of what later became the Second Helvetic Confession of 1562 and revised it in 1564 when the plague was raging in Zurich. Believing that he would not survive its ravages, he set forth his personal confession of faith and added it to his last will and testament, all of which was to be turned over to the magistrate in Zurich in the event of his death. When the request came from Frederick in Heidelberg for help in preparing his defense for his heresy trial, this was the confession of faith that Bullinger sent. A long document (the longest of the eleven statements in the *Book of Confessions*), it resembles the early *Institutes* of John Calvin and expresses a similar theology. Its faith is set out in thirty major theological statements.

It begins, like most Reformation documents, with a statement about Scripture: Scripture, which is the Word of God, contains all that pertains to a saving faith and to a godly life. God alone proclaims what is true and what is false, what is to be followed and what avoided.

God is described in trinitarian terms, as one in essence but revealed in a threefold manner, each person co-substantial, co-eternal, and co-equal. God has providentially appointed everything to its end as well as the means by which it reaches its goal. Therefore the faithful need not be anxious about anything.

God created all things, but humans used their free will to become immersed in perverse desires. Only through Christ, offered through the predestination of God, does salvation come.

Christ, true God and true man, the only Savior of humankind, through his death and resurrection reconciled the faithful to the heavenly Father, made expiation for sins, disarmed death, overcame damnation and hell, restored life and immortality. All humanity needs to give glory to Christ and rest in him alone.

While the law of God works wrath and announces a curse, the gospel preaches grace and blessing, offering the earthly promises of daily bread and the eternal promises of remission of sin and eternal life through faith in Christ. The Christian life begins in repentance and conversion, justification by faith, and moves on to faith and the good works that proceed from faith.

The church, the community of those who know and rightly worship the true God in Christ, wages war on earth against sin, death, and the devil, and triumphs in heaven after having overcome all these. The sacraments, given by God, present to us Christ the Savior. In Baptism persons are enrolled in the holy family of God; in the Lord's Supper we give thanks for our redemption and receive Christ by faith that he may live in us and we in him.

Civil governance—the last of the sections of the confession—is, said Bullinger, instituted by God for the peace and tranquillity of the human race, and citizens are to honor magistrates as ministers of God. They are to obey their just and fair commands, pay all customs and taxes faithfully and willingly, even lay down their lives if necessary for the public safety. The confession closes with this prayer:

> We beseech God, our most merciful Father in heaven, that he will bless the rulers of the people, and us, and his whole people, through Jesus Christ, our only Lord and Savior; to whom be praise and glory and thanksgiving, for all ages. Amen. (5.260)

A few concluding remarks about the Second Helvetic Confession are in order.

1. Bullinger, in calling attention to the language and circumstances in which Scripture was written, opened the way for careful and critical scholarship concerning the Bible. In doing this he was being true to the Swiss Reformation, which produced scholars like Calvin, Beza, and himself and which has placed all persons of Reformed faith under the obligation to follow their lead.

2. He presented a very moderate position on predestination. Whereas John Calvin increasingly leaned toward double predestination (God predestining some to eternal life but others to eternal death), Bullinger spoke only of the predestination of love and held that if we are in Christ there can be no doubt about our election.

3. The lengthiest sections of the confession, and those presumably most important in the author's own thinking, center upon Christ and his meaning for human life; our justification by grace through faith in Christ; and the church, its sacraments and its ministry, which make known to the world the good news of this gospel.

4. He presented a stirring section on the ministry of the church, to which he had given a great deal of thought. The

minister—a person of consecrated learning, pious elo-
quence, simple wisdom, and honorable reputation—is called
to teach the gospel of Christ and to administer the sacraments properly. Ministers are to comfort and strengthen the
fainthearted; rebuke offenders; recall the erring; raise the
fallen; prepare people by wholesome doctrine to receive the
sacraments; catechize the unlearned; commend the needs of
the poor to the church; visit the sick and those afflicted with
various temptations; and see to everything that makes for the
tranquillity, peace, and welfare of the churches. To accomplish this, the minister is to fear God, be constant in prayer,
attend to spiritual reading, and at all times be watchful.
Bullinger's description of ministry is nearly a job description
for the pastor of our day.

5. The sacraments were very important to him, because
through them Christ still works within us. Baptism provides
for our inward purification and renewal; through his Supper
the Lord keeps in our fresh remembrance his sacrifice by
which he has pardoned our sins, has redeemed us from
eternal death and the power of evil, and now nourishes us
to eternal life when we participate in this meal through faith.
Bullinger, the pastor and preacher, the leader of his congregation's worship, leads us to think through with him the
deep meanings of these sacred acts.

6. Like other Reformation leaders, Bullinger gave careful
thought to the relation between church and state. He saw
civil government and civil leaders as part of God's gift of
tranquillity and order. He instructed the congregation in
Zurich in good citizenship, and as one who filled a pulpit
formerly held by a clergyman killed in battle protecting his
city's freedom, he made a place in his thinking for the concept of the "just and mournful war." Having seen at close
hand the destabilizing of sixteenth-century society that had
occurred in the peasants' revolts and in the civil disobedi-
ence of the Anabaptists, he was opposed to revolt and rebel-
lion as a means of social change and he prayed that such a
means would never be necessary. Like all Reformers, he

knew that church and state had to coexist in this life as well as within the will of God, and his thinking, along with that of his contemporaries, has helped to direct the way Presbyterians in the twentieth century have dealt with the issue.

The Second Helvetic Confession, important in its own time, continues to provide the church with the basics of the Presbyterian lifestyle and calls us to further consideration of the meaning of our own Christian faith.

3
The Westminster Documents

The Westminster documents come from a generation that is removed by a century and more from the Reformation.

It could be said that the world of the seventeenth century was divided into two parts, one Catholic, the other Protestant. In 1588 the Spanish Armada was sent to invade England, and was defeated. It was the last vast attempt by Catholic Europe to win Protestant Europe back to itself, and it had failed. From that time until the twentieth century, what was Catholic remained Catholic and what was Protestant remained Protestant.

But people then did not know that, so England was constantly being alerted to the possibility of a Catholic takeover, and was constantly on guard lest a king convert to Catholicism and lead England back into the arms of France. The Protestants in England themselves did not know what direction they would take: toward Anglicanism, as their kings seemed to want; toward Presbyterianism, as the people in Parliament seemed to want; or toward Independency, with neither king nor Parliament having the final say in the affairs of church, province, city, or village. When the Westminster documents were being written, the people and their rulers in England had not yet made a final decision.

The Westminster divines thought they were making the decision in favor of Parliament's Presbyterian position, and they wrote their statements from that point of view. In fact, they were hardly willing to recognize that there were any answers other than their own to the questions of the day, and their documents reflect this attitude. It could be said that they prepared statements of fact rather than articles of belief. Dealing with many of the same questions as did the reformers, they brought to them the insights that had been worked out in the eighty years since Calvin's death and reformulated questions and answers in the light of their own experience. What they accomplished in those short years satisfied Presbyterians the world over for many generations, and yet theological questions continue to be raised in every generation. Their work deserves our careful study.

The Westminster Confession of Faith

Civil war embroiled England while the Westminster Assembly was in session. Armies roamed highways and back roads, families chose up sides, estates were devastated, churches despoiled, farms, fields, and towns decimated, people died, and the Westminster Assembly sat, talked, debated, wrote—sat, talked, debated—sat . . . .

On May 13, 1643, an ordinance was introduced into the British House of Commons calling for the "settling of the government and liturgy of the Church of England, [in a manner] most agreeable to God's Holy Word and most apt to procure . . . the peace of the church at home, and nearer agreement with the Church of Scotland and other Reformed Churches abroad."[9] On June 12, the same ordinance passed the House of Lords. The meeting to accomplish this formidable task was called to begin on July 1 of the same year.

One hundred fifty-one persons were nominated to the Assembly by Parliament, 121 of whom were "learned, godly, and judicious divines." The other thirty were members of the two houses of Parliament. Dr. William Twisse of Newberry was appointed Moderator (Prolocutor). A sum of four shillings a day was allowed each man (there were no women members of the Assembly) to defray his expenses. All were freed from penalty of nonresidence or absence from their churches. (This was important; some members were absent as long as six years from their normal vocations; the attrition of church life in the British Isles caused by the mere "sitting" of this Assembly was one of its least positive effects and may in part have contributed to the collapse of the Presbyterian position in Great Britain during the Restoration.) Five Scottish emissaries, the very elite of the Scottish clergy, were attached to the Assembly with the right of discussion but not of vote. Invitations to send delegates were sent to churches in Holland, Belgium, France, Switzerland, and the American colonies, but no one came. The Assembly held 1,163 sessions until it ceased its meetings on February 22, 1649, even though it continued to meet informally and in committees for three more years. Richard Baxter, a leading contemporary churchman who was not invited to the Assembly, said of its members, "The divines there congregated were men of eminent learning, godliness, ministerial abilities, and fidelity. . . . As far as I am able to judge . . . the Christian world, since the days of the apostles, had never a synod of more excellent divines."[10]

It is good that they were able and sensitive men, for the task confronting them was formidable indeed. The past forty years under King James I and his son Charles I had been a time of great internal conflict in England. There were vast theological problems whose roots went back to the Reformation and to the various revisions of the Book of Prayer of the Church of England. At issue also was the political question of rule and authority: what power should the king have, what power Parliament? By and large the Anglican party stood for monarchical church government with primary authority vested in the king. The Presbyterian party sought to vest authority in duly elected representatives of the people. James himself, a Stuart from Scotland sympathetic to Calvinist doctrine (and known to us as the man who authorized the "King James Version" of the Bible), drew the line at the point of Presbyterian polity which would have undercut his royal position. After his death his son and successor, Charles I, appointed William Laud to be Archbishop of Canterbury, and together they attempted to root out the Presbyterianism that had remained strong in Ireland and

Scotland. In 1641 an insurrection took place in Ireland, and Scottish and English Presbyterians leaped to support their brothers. Civil war also began in England. Parliament—the famous "Long Parliament," which met on November 3, 1640, and continued until dissolved by Cromwell in 1652—issued a call in 1642 for a "Westminster Assembly" to deal with these problems. The call was frustrated by the objections of Charles I, but the Assembly finally sat, despite the objections of the king, in 1643.

During most of its life the Assembly was not representative of the divisions in the Church of England. Four Anglican bishops had been elected by Parliament to attend, but because King Charles considered attendance at the Assembly to be an act of disloyalty to him, they chose not to be present. Five to twelve Independents, from the party of Oliver Cromwell, attended and argued vigorously against forming presbyteries and synods. They believed that every congregation should be able to govern itself without interference. Yet another group, the Erastians, were represented in the Assembly. They asserted the supremacy of civil government in all matters of church discipline and would, in effect, have made the church a department of the state. Both Independents and Erastians withdrew from the Assembly before the adoption of the Book of Discipline in 1647. Even the Scottish commissioners had given up their seats by the end of that year, leaving the Assembly fully in the hands of the largest party, the Presbyterians. Had the others remained, the final documents that came from the Assembly might have been quite different. As it was, the Assembly produced standards of theology and polity that were self-consciously and intentionally Presbyterian.

Despite the vast difficulties confronting the Assembly, the work they accomplished was of major stature. Shortly after it convened, the Assembly received and adopted a document called the "Solemn League and Covenant," already agreed to between the Scottish General Assembly and the English deputation sent to Scotland. This league was for "the peace and safety of the three kingdoms," and the signers pledged to work for "the preservation of the reformed religion in Scotland and the reformation of religion in England and Ireland." This was adopted on September 25, 1643. By the end of 1644, the Assembly had completed the "Form of Presbyterian Church Government" (the first work attempted, since the question of authority was the chief one before the Assembly), and the "Directory of Public Worship." In April, October, and November, 1647, "The Confession of Faith," "The Larger Catechism," and "The Shorter Catechism" were completed, in that order. Civil war or no, these divines stayed with their work.

The Assembly came to a peculiar end. In one sense, it finished its work and had no further reason to meet. During the four years of its life, it had restated the position of the Reformed faith in a way that would essentially determine Presbyterian life and thought for the next three hundred years, an admirable work. In another sense, it did not complete its task. It did not succeed in reforming the Church of England or in reuniting the churches of the Reformed faith, though it stayed in session a full two years after it had completed its work of restatement in the fond but futile hope that it could yet accomplish this larger task.

Cromwell's ascendancy was the blow that ended the Assembly. Pride's Purge, December 6, 1648—the forcible exclusion of the Presbyterian members from Parliament—was a major blow. Even more decisive was the execution of Charles I on January 29, 1649, an act that appalled the Presbyterians and caused them to protest. This protest, plus their insistence on ordered and representative church government responsible to itself and not to the state, brought the wrath of Cromwell upon the Presbyterians, and English Puritanism was irrevocably split into "Presbyterians" and "Independents." In England the work of the Assembly fell into disrepute.

It was through Scotland that the product of the Assembly had lasting effect. The Scots General Assembly adopted the Westminster Standards for use in the kirk (they replaced the Scots Confession of 1560, the Heidelberg Catechism, and the Second Helvetic Confession), and missionaries from the kirk carried these documents to America. In 1729 they were adopted as the confessional position of the newly organized Presbyterian synod in the colonies, and have since played a formative role in the life of American Presbyterianism.

The Westminster Confession of Faith, the key theological document, is a breathtaking statement that speaks of God's work from its beginning in creation to its end in resurrection and last judgment. God, insists the confession, is first and last and preeminent in all things. The task of humankind is to understand God in all God's creation and to bring our lives into accord with God's magnificent will.

So the confession begins with God's self-revelation in Scripture, for, while "nature and the works of creation and providence" so reveal God "as to leave [us] inexcusable; yet are they not sufficient to give that knowledge of God, and of his will, which is necessary unto salvation" (6.001). Only Scripture does that: In Scripture, God reveals his will to the church and has committed the same to writing (6.001), the authority for which depends not on the testimony of any person or institution "but wholly upon God (who is truth itself), the author thereof" (6.004).

Who is this God?

There is but one only living and true God, who is infinite in being and perfection, a most pure spirit, invisible, without body, parts, or passions, immutable, immense, eternal, incomprehensible, almighty, most wise, most holy, most free, most absolute, working all things according to the counsel of his own immutable and most righteous will, for his own glory; most loving, gracious, merciful, long-suffering, abundant in goodness and truth, forgiving iniquity, transgression, and sin; the rewarder of them that diligently seek him; and withal most just and terrible in his judgments, hating all sin, and who will by no means clear the guilty. (6.011)

Knowledge of God in the Westminster Confession is cognitive and contemplative; the confession calls us to stand in awe before the majesty of the Almighty.

This God is able to decree whatever God wills, as the confession clearly states: "God from all eternity did . . . freely and unchangeably decree whatsoever comes to pass. . . . By the decree of God, . . . some men and angels are predestined to everlasting life, and others fore-ordained to everlasting death. . . . Those of mankind that are predestined unto life, God . . . hath chosen in Christ . . . to the praise of his glorious grace. . . . The rest of mankind, God . . . [ordained] . . . to dishonor and wrath for their sin, to the praise of his glorious justice" (6.014, .016, .018, .020).

This awesome prolegomena is a preparation for the remainder of the confession. Having portrayed the scene in the heavens of God's will, the confession moves to the earth to witness this will working itself out. God created all things out of nothing, says the document, and this includes humankind, whom God upholds, directs, and governs. But human beings did not remain in blessed harmony with the will and purpose of God. Human sin intervened, which God permitted but did not cause, and out of that act came a defilement that extends to all people and from which all actual transgressions proceed. This corruption, states the confession, remains in this life, even after we are regenerated by Christ, and each sin brings its own guilt upon the sinner.

But God has not left us in this fallen state. God made a covenant of grace with humankind. Perfectly seen in Jesus Christ, this covenant was foreshadowed in the Old Testament and fulfilled in the New. Christ is the mediator between God and humankind; the prophet, priest, and king; head and savior of his church; heir of all things and judge of the world.

Can we enter of our own free will into the covenant of grace? The Westminster divines could not say so; that was contrary to their understanding that God has the prerogative to choose whom God pleased. If humans have free will, they asserted, it existed only in a state of innocence that is long passed; in this world each person is a compound of free choices and determined responses. The Christian, they said, has the ability to respond to the grace and judgment of God that is present in each decision confronting us, but even the Christian is not free in all decisions to choose the good and only the good, and in this life we never shall be. God is the chooser and we are the responders; we cannot probe the mystery deeper than that.

But the Christian life is a life of grace and glory. The Christian is justified, adopted, sanctified, granted a saving faith, and repents of sins. Faith "is the gift of God. . . . Thus receiving and resting on Christ and his righteousness, [faith] . . . is the alone instrument of justification" (6.068, .069). "All those that are justified . . . enjoy the liberties and privileges of the children of God; have his name put upon them; receive the spirit of adoption; have access to the throne of grace with boldness; are enabled to cry, Abba, Father; are pitied, protected, provided for, and chastened by him as a father; yet never cast off, but sealed to the day of redemption, and inherit the promises, as heirs of everlasting salvation" (6.074). "The grace of faith . . . is the work of the spirit of Christ in [our] hearts."

Neither the stress of the times nor the harshness of their doctrine can obscure the joy in the hearts of the men of Westminster over the wonder of Christ and the grace of God in granting Christ to us.

But problems remain, in the interior life and in its public expression.

What about those devout Christians who inwardly wonder about the reality of what they believe? The confession replies: "Infallible assurance doth not so belong to the essence of faith but that a true believer may wait long . . . before he be partaker of it" (6.099). Our assurance is the assurance of faith, not verifiable fact. The essence of the Christian life is true commitment to the Lord Jesus Christ, a sincere love for him, and an endeavor to walk in good conscience before him. It is faithless to ask for other signs, wonders, verifications, and assurances.

What about those public matters that were upsetting the realm and tearing apart the fabric of English life? "God alone is Lord of the conscience," said the confession, "and hath left it free from the doctrines and commandments of men which are in anything contrary to his Word, or beside it in matters of faith or worship" (6.109). This statement was a call to arms sounded before any tyranny, religious or political, that existed in England in 1647. In the next paragraphs the innate conservatism of the Reformed movement showed itself. "Because the powers which God hath ordained, and the liberty which Christ hath purchased, are not intended by God to destroy, but mutually to uphold and preserve one another; they who, upon pretense of Christian liberty, shall oppose any lawful power, . . . whether it be civil or ecclesiastical, resist the ordinance of God" (6.111). Appalled by the growing Cromwellian revolt and wanting no part of it, the Presbyterians wrote into their confession that they fully believed that God had established kings and kingdoms—what they termed "civil magistrates"— to preserve order and to protect the church, and that any attack upon these was treasonable not only to the civil authority but to God. The summons to liberty of conscience is set in the context of a social order that is part of the eternal plan of Almighty God. The dilemma of the Presbyterian conscience as regards civil matters is summarized in these two conflicting statements.

Church and sacraments are the last matters considered in the confession, since these ordinances stand at the junction of earth and heaven. The human institution of the church, subject to all the sins and faults human life is heir to, points beyond itself to the life to come and the goal of all God's work of creation and redemption. The church invisible is defined as "the whole number of the elect, that have been, are, or shall be gathered into one, under Christ" (6.140). The church visible, with its "ministry, oracles, and ordinances of God [is] for the gathering and perfecting of the saints in this life" (6.142). The church is "sometimes more, sometimes less, visible" (6.143); that is, the perfect church exists somewhere in the perfection of God but is seen only here and there in the real life of the world.

But the end is before us, the end of all things and the goal of God's working. "Then shall the righteous go into everlasting life, and receive that fullness of joy and refreshing which shall come from the presence of the Lord: but the wicked, who know not God, and obey not the gospel of Jesus Christ, shall be cast into eternal torments" (6.181). God has appointed a day in which the world shall be judged in righteousness. On this day, God shall manifest the glory of God's mercy in the eternal salvation of the elect; and of God's justice, in the damnation of the reprobate. The key lies in the person's response to the gospel of Jesus Christ. Since no one knows the day, all need to "be always watchful . . . and may be ever prepared to say, Come, Lord Jesus, come quickly" (6.182).

The Catechisms

Two additional theological documents were prepared to accompany the confession. The Larger Catechism, written primarily by Dr. Anthony Tuckney, professor of divinity and vice-chancellor of Cambridge University, was designed for public exposition from the pulpit. The Shorter Catechism, which may be traced to the work of the Rev. John Wallis, an eminent mathematician who later became professor of geometry at Oxford, was directed toward the education of children. Unlike most earlier catechisms, neither contained a section on the Apostles' Creed, but both deal with questions of God, Christ, the Christian life, the Ten Commandments, the sacraments, and the Lord's Prayer.

The section of the Larger Catechism dealing with the sacraments is most important.

"How is our baptism to be improved by us?" This quaintly phrased question indicates not only that baptism is a once-for-all act but that it has implications which remain with the believer throughout his or her Christian life. In time of temptation, answers the catechism, and during the time we witness the administration of baptism to others, we are to consider its nature and purpose; remember the solemn vow made in our behalf at the time of our baptism; recall the way we have failed to live up to the vow; accept anew the pardon of sins offered through it; draw strength from the crucified and resurrected Christ whose grace is offered to us; and resolve again to endeavor to walk in faith. The statement about "improving baptism" has two immediate effects: since our baptism needs to be "improved," it opens the way for a theology of Christian education; and it points to the truly sacramental nature of baptism, in that not only does the one baptized receive the grace offered but the whole congregation participates in receiving that grace. Those present at baptism are not merely spectators but participants who are to give "serious and thankful consideration" for that which is being performed and hence are to receive anew the sacramental grace "in faith."

The questions designed to aid the Christian in participation in the Lord's Supper are also significant.

Question 171 reminds us that we are to examine ourselves—our sins, our wants, our Christian knowledge, faith, repentance, love to God, charity to God's people, the depth of our forgiveness of others, our obedience to Christ—before we partake of the Lord's Supper.

Answer 174 reminds us that when we are present at the Lord's Supper we are to watch what is being done, listen to what is being said, meditate upon the death and sufferings of Christ, judge ourselves against him, sorrow for our sins, feed on Christ by faith, receive his fullness and trust his sufficiency, rejoice in his love, give thanks for his grace, and once more renew our covenant with God.

Question 172 is also important: if you have serious questions about the meaning of the sacrament, or if you question the quality of your own Christian life, ought you to come to the Table of the Lord? The answer is a reassuring "Yes." The questioning itself indicates the seriousness with which we are examining our Christian life, and this seriousness is already pointing us to Christ. We are therefore to come—bewailing our unbelief, laboring to have doubts resolved—"that [we] may be further strengthened." Such statements point to the peak of pastoral concern that marked English Puritanism at its best.

Statements from the Shorter Catechism have also helped to mold Christian life. Question 3 gives us the outline of the catechism and defines the system of doctrine to which Presbyterians have adhered for three centuries: "The Scriptures principally teach what man is to believe concerning God, and what duty God requires of man." Questions 23–26 speak of the threefold work of Christ as prophet, priest, and king. The definition given in Question 98 has helped to develop the Christian's prayer life: "Prayer is an offering up of our desires unto God, for things agreeable to his will, in the name of Christ, with confession of our sins and thankful acknowledgment of his mercies."

The greatest contribution of the Shorter Catechism, perhaps, lies in its first question, "What is the chief end of man?" "Man's chief end is to glorify God, and to enjoy him forever." "Enjoy" refers to the meaning given it originally by the great Christian thinker Augustine. "How does one regard God?" asked Augustine twelve hundred years before Westminster. "Are we to seek him for what he can do for us, or as someone to be loved for his own sake?" Then Augustine answered his own question, "We are not to use God for our own purposes; we are to enjoy God for his own sake." The Westminster Assembly picked up the word: God is to be "enjoyed," that is, loved unconditionally, for who God is. Proper love of God puts God at the center of everything, one's own life, the nation's existence, the world's, all God's creation.

When the General Assembly of the Church of Scotland, after careful examination, adopted the Westminster Standards at Edinburgh on August 27, 1647, they declared them "to be most agreeable to the Word of God," and they thankfully acknowledged the great mercy of God "in that so excellent a Confession of Faith is prepared." The Westminster Standards are indeed remarkable documents. In scope, they embrace the total field of theology, from God's eternal decrees to God's final judgment; in influence, they exceed all other Protestant documents in their effect upon Christian churches and Christian people.

But the work of Westminster represented the end of a theological era as well as a beginning. The Assembly was heir to a tradition that extended back through Bullinger and Knox to Calvin. Behind these men stood Augustine of Hippo, the fifth-century bishop who was one of the greatest theologians of western Christendom. But, like Augustine who witnessed the breakup of the Roman empire and who tried to make sense of it in his theological magnum opus *The City of God,* the Westminster Assembly gathered in a time of cosmic convulsion. Not only was there civil turmoil, strife, and warfare; a cultural revolution was also in the making. Galileo and Copernicus had opened new vistas into the physical universe. Descartes and Hobbes were asking disturbing questions in philosophy. Shakespeare's work was over, and in the dramatists who followed him it was clear that the medieval unities that gave his work form and meaning had already disappeared. The new worlds of the Americas were opening up, and strange worlds of the East were becoming known. The cultural situation was one of breakup, confusion, explosion. The world of the Renaissance and the Reformation was at an end, and no one could predict what would emerge. Before this era ended, however, the Westminster Confession and its companion papers formulated in an encompassing manner the faith of the Reformed and Presbyterian churches and assisted people of future generations to withstand the stresses and storms that were to engulf them.

4
Contemporary Confessions

What can we say about the twentieth century, that era of which—for better or for worse—we are God's stewards?

It has been the bloodiest century in history. No other hundred years has seen so many people die in warfare, so many lands destroyed.

It has been the most revolutionary of centuries. The face of the globe has been remade again and again as countries rise and fall and political entities and persons come and go.

It has seen the rise of new technologies with their promises and their problems. Glowing expectations and glowering frustration confront each other.

It has seen the population of the earth double and redouble. It has seen the sum total of human knowledge grow geometrically.

It has brooding over it the capability of nuclear catastrophe that could turn the planet into a cinder in the twinkling of an eye.

It has thrust us into the future faster than we were meant to go or wished to go.

How does the Christian respond to this century? By organizing churches and denominations, harnessing the means of communication, and designing mission projects. That is part of our response. By suffering and dying for the faith, as in Armenia, then Germany and the rest of Europe, then Russia, then China, then Central and South America, then Africa and South Africa in particular. Ours is the century of martyrs; for sheer numbers of martyrdoms no previous century has matched our own. And we have responded to our times by writing confessions as rallying points for the faithful. Since the turn of the century more than thirty such confessional statements have been written in the Reformed branch of Christianity alone.

Of these our church includes three in the *Book of Confessions*. One came from the days when persecution and martyrdom seemed more a thing of the past than of the future. In the 1920s Germany could recall the heroic age of the church when people actually died for their faith, but none of that generation thought they would see such a time again, certainly not in civilized Germany! Then came Hitler with his idolatries of state and flag and race, and his challenge to the church. The church, totally unprepared for this pagan onslaught, had to make a response. The Barmen Confession was part of what it did.

When the Second World War was over, and the revolution of rising expectations was affecting Western Europe and the United States, all the problems seemed to be swept away in the face of economic prosperity and political calm. Then in the United States blacks and other ethnic groups began to point out that life certainly was not well with them; and students began to fight against being filed away like forgotten computer cards; and wars occurring in faraway jungles swallowed up American troops; and women began to say aloud what they had known for centuries, that men had organized society for their own benefit; and suppressed peoples began to clamor for the right to live their own lives; and John F. Kennedy was killed, as were Martin Luther King Jr., and Robert F. Kennedy, and a whole generation might smile again but would never be young again. Suddenly the world was filled with problems clamoring to be solved.

In Rome, Pope John XXIII called for a council of the Roman Catholic Church to frame its response to issues being raised in the world. His devoted counselors thought his call would unnecessarily disturb the church. "Why call a council now?" they anxiously asked. *"Aggiornamento,"* he would say in

Italian, which, roughly translated, means "updating, bringing the church up to date with the world around." In the United States the Presbyterians were not using the word, but they were doing the same thing. The result was the Confession of 1967, and it too was added to the *Book of Confessions.* A third, A Brief Statement of Faith, was added in 1991.

The Theological Declaration of Barmen

In response to the rise of Nazism, the Reformed and Lutheran churches of Germany—a portion of them, at least—met in synod at the city of Barmen in May 1934. They met to consider the adoption of a statement, written largely by the Swiss theologian Karl Barth, which declared the church's opposition to the policies of Hitler's National Socialist (Nazi) Party.

When Hitler came to power most of the German people were unprepared for what was about to happen. Germany— with its universities, its music and drama and literature, its free press and democratic institutions—was, in the minds of most Germans, the very epitome of an enlightened nation, and though some of the people had read of Hitler's savage policies in his book *Mein Kampf* (My Struggle), hardly anyone believed that he would be able to put them into effect.

With astonishing rapidity he did just that. He established his party in 1919 at the end of the tragic First World War, and by 1928, Hitler and his followers had gained twelve seats in the Reichstag. Riding the wave of worldwide depression, the Nazis increased that number to 107 by 1930, and by the time of the elections in July 1932, Hitler's party was the largest in the nation. And in January 1933, Hitler was named chancellor of Germany. Since the Nazis still did not have a majority of the seats in the Reichstag, Hitler called a new election for March 1933. On the night of February 27, 1933, the Reichstag building was set afire and burned. Although the arson was the work of the Nazis, Hitler blamed the Communists and used the incident as the occasion for issuing, the day after the fire, a decree that abolished all human rights and democratic processes in government. Under this edict, police could arrest and detain anyone without a hearing, keep people in prison for an indefinite period without trial, search private dwellings without a warrant, seize property, censor or prohibit publication of newspapers and books, tap telephones, forbid meetings, dissolve political parties. The results of four hundred years of struggle in Europe for civil and human rights disappeared in a single night.

In rapid order Hitler outlawed all political parties other than the Nazis; smashed the labor unions by arresting their leaders and confiscating their properties; murdered opposition leaders within his own party; organized the young people of the nation into the "Hitler Youth"; purged the universities of the leading liberal teachers; replaced the German system of jurisprudence with a "People's Court" that followed his own dictates; began his systematic terrorism of the Jewish people; and tried to reorganize the Christian church in a manner that combined Christianity with the tenets of National Socialism. All these changes were in effect by the fall of 1933, scarcely eight months after Hitler had originally taken power.

Hitler's policy toward the church was twofold: he wanted to eliminate political Catholicism by working out an agreement with the Vatican, and he wanted quickly to establish a National German Evangelical Church. He achieved the first objective by July 20, 1933, when he reached a concordat between the Holy See and the German Reich (state) that prohibited church officers from membership in political parties. He moved toward the second on September 27 of the same year, when he appointed his lackey, Ludwig Müller, as Reich Bishop and moved to take over the apparatus of the Protestant churches.

The churches fought back. Under pressure from the Catholic bishops of Munich, Berlin, Cologne, Breslau, and Münster, the pope was persuaded that Nazism was as blatant an enemy of the Christian faith as was Communism, and on March 4, 1937, he issued an encyclical that constituted an outright repudiation of Nazism. The response of the Protestants was different but they became equally outspoken in their opposition to the Nazis.

Protestantism in Germany, like the other institutions of German life, was unprepared to meet the Nazi onslaught. When Hitler came to power, dynamic church life was almost nonexistent. While nearly everyone was baptized and confirmed, married and buried by the church, attendance at worship was good at the Christmas and Easter seasons, but at other times the churches were empty. The union of Christianity, nationalism, and militarism was taken for granted; patriotic sentiments were equated with Christian truth. Hitler was able to build upon this attitude, and he supported the establishment of a "German Christian" church which identified Christianity with National Socialism and said that the exaltation of "race, folk, and nation" was the will of God revealed to the German people. The "Guiding Principles" of the movement were stated on June 6, 1932, and included the following:

4. We take our stand upon the ground of positive Christianity. We profess an affirmative and typical faith in Christ, corresponding to the German spirit of Luther and to a heroic piety.

6. We demand . . . that a fight be waged against . . . Marxism . . . and against its Christian social fellow travelers of every shade. . . .

7. We see in race, folk, and nation, orders of existence granted and entrusted to us by God. God's law for us is that we look to the preservation of these orders. . . .

10. We want an evangelical Church that is rooted in our nationhood. We repudiate the spirit of a Christian world-citizenship. We want the degenerating manifestations of this spirit, such as pacifism, internationalism, Free Masonry, etc., overcome by a faith in our national mission that God has committed to us.[11]

With uncanny skill in political maneuvering, Hitler succeeded in getting most of the superintendents of the German church to agree with these principles and with the appointment of Ludwig Müller to be head of the church. Hitler was now ready to use even the Christian church for his heathen purposes. Not all churches joined in the "German Christian" movement. On January 11, 1933, twenty-one pastors at Altona, led by the courageous and articulate Hans Asmussen, issued a statement declaring that the task of the church is to sharpen the conscience as it proclaims the gospel and that the church is permitting itself to be misused when it is made the stage for military, political, and party celebration and when it approves any particular economic system, political party, or military service. On September 21, Martin Niemöller, pastor of the Dahlem Church in Berlin, sent a letter to all pastors in Germany inviting them to join the Pastors' Emergency League and to pledge to "execute my office as minister of the World, holding myself bound solely to Holy Scripture and to the Confessions of the Reformation as the true exposition of Holy Scripture."[12] Thirteen hundred pastors immediately signed, and by January 15, 1934, there were 7,036 members of the league. On January 4, 1934, Reich Bishop Müller issued an order, later known as the Muzzling Order, forbidding ministers to introduce into their sermons any reference to the issues facing the churches. Four thousand pastors read the letter from their pulpits the next Sunday and publicly deplored the order.

By this time, assemblies of all sorts were being held in Germany, the most notable being at Ulm on April 22, 1934, when the assembly decreed:

> There is violence and injustice against which all true Christians must pray and bear witness to the Word. As a fellowship of determined fighters obedient to the Lord Jesus Christ, we pray Almighty God to open the eyes of all Christians to the danger that threatens our beloved Church. May he not let us waver in remaining faithful to his honor and in his service. May we also do all that he

requires of us in loyalty and service to our nation and
State. . . . You Christians who speak the German tongue,
stand together with us all, firmly grounded upon God's
Word, constant in prayer, joyful in faith and love! Then
this day will bring a blessing upon our whole Church and
our whole nation. God grant it![13]

Since these synods and assemblies had involved sectors of
the church only and not the whole church, leaders of the
movement, especially Asmussen, Niemöller, and Barth, began
to consider calling a synod of all Lutheran, Reformed, and
United churches of Germany, who could confess their faith
with one voice and spirit. The synod was to meet in the city
of Barmen, Tuesday through Thursday, May 29–31, 1934,
with Pastor Karl K. Immer making the local arrangements.
Asmussen, Barth, and Thomas Breit were appointed to draw
up a theological statement that the synod could discuss. Barth
was the author of the first draft of the statement, writing it out
by hand on the afternoon of May 16. Changes were made in
the statement by the Committee of Three, but at the synod
meeting on May 30, the changes were deleted and the final
draft was very close to the original.

The format of the meeting of the Barmen synod would be
familiar to anyone who has attended a presbytery or synod
meeting in any church. One hundred thirty-nine delegates
drawn from eighteen judicatories and representing Lutheran,
Reformed, and United churches were in attendance. Fifty-
three delegates were laymen, and six university professors
were also included. Only one woman was a delegate. The
average age of the group was barely forty years. Karl Koch of
Bad-Oeynhausen presided. The synod was constituted with the
worship service on the evening of Tuesday, May 29, in the
Gemarke Church in Barmen, which was filled to overflowing.
The report of the theological committee was made the next
morning by Pastor Hans Asmussen, who read and explained
the report. The synod then divided, Lutherans meeting with
Lutherans, Reformed with Reformed, to discuss the statement.

A committee representing both communions was appointed to rework the declaration. Their report was brought to the floor of the synod on Thursday morning, May 31, when it was discussed at length. Shortly before 1:00 P.M. the declaration was adopted unanimously (the one delegate who was opposed had explained his reason for opposition and had left the synod). The assembly rose to sing "Now Thank We All Our God," and then it recessed for lunch. The meeting concluded in the late afternoon.

The Barmen Declaration begins with an appeal to the Evangelical Congregations in Germany and then states the theological situation as seen from its perspective. Six theses follow that make up the heart of the document. Each thesis consists of an appropriate quotation from Scripture, draws the positive implications of this Scripture passage for the situation of the church at that time, and then sets forth an "anathema" by which the position of the German Christian party was castigated. The heart of the declaration is found in its first two theses.

The first thesis begins: "I am the way, and the truth, and the life; no one comes to the Father, but by me" (John 14:6). This means, says the declaration, that "Jesus Christ, as he is attested for us in Holy Scripture, is the one Word of God which we have to hear and which we have to trust and obey in life and in death" (8.10–.11).

The second thesis begins: "Christ Jesus, whom God made our wisdom, our righteousness and sanctification and redemption" (1 Cor. 1:30). The text continues: "As Jesus Christ is God's assurance of the forgiveness of our sins, so in the same way and with the same seriousness he is also God's mighty claim upon our whole life. Through him befalls us a joyful deliverance from the godless fetters of this world for a free, grateful service to his creatures" (8.13–.14).

In explaining this thesis, Pastor Asmussen said to the assembly:

[Christ] does not simply translate us from sin into a state of grace, then leave us to ourselves, but . . . he redeems us from godlessness and sin in order that we may belong to him and live *subject* to him, and so that his presence constantly confronts us in the life he has given us as a judging and saving claim. . . . Thus we freely and gratefully serve him and his creatures. . . . What we fear more than death is the fact that God's creatures and events in history lead us into . . . the temptation to seek God *without Christ* from and in the creatures and events. Whenever that happens, whether under a pagan or Christian guise, there exist man's own wisdom, his self-righteousness, self-sanctification, self-redemption. Other lords than Jesus Christ, other commandments than his commandments, acquire dominion over us. They offer their services to us as saviors, but they prove to be torturers of an unredeemed world. . . . We warn everyone against the misuse of the divine offer whereby one wants to have the assurance of the forgiveness of sins but rejects God's claim on the ground of the forgiveness of sins.[14]

Statement 5, built on 1 Peter 2:17, "Fear God. Honor the emperor," also spoke to their situation. Said Asmussen,

Scripture tells us that, in the as yet unredeemed world in which the Church also exists, the State has by divine appointment the task of providing for justice and peace. [It fulfills that task] by means of the threat and exercise of force, according to the measure of human judgment and human ability. The Church acknowledges the benefit of this divine appointment in gratitude and reverence toward him. . . .

[But] State and Church are both bound, the latter in the realm of the gospel, the former in the realm of law, . . . Any infringement of their respective obligation leads to a servitude that is alien to the nature of either Church or State. . . . When the State proclaims an eternal kingdom, an eternal law, and an eternal righteousness, it corrupts itself and with it its people. When the Church preaches a political kingdom, an earthly law, and the justice of a human form of society, it goes beyond its limits and drags the State down into the mire with it.[15]

The final statement of the declaration, drawing upon the promise of Jesus Christ to be with his church always, to the close of the age, calls upon the church to deliver its message of the free grace of God to all people in Christ's stead. Once more Pastor Asmussen delivered the official interpretation of the statement:

[In the fellowship of the church] Christ lives, works, and rules, not simply as an idea but as the living Lord, not simply in an unattainable distance but right in our midst. . . . It is the urgent task of the Church to express through visible signs that instruction by the Holy Spirit and the presence of Christ are not desirable ideals for the Church but a starting point given to it for its action in word and deed.[16]

The Barmen Declaration accomplished many things. It tied together Reformed and Lutheran doctrine. It stood in the Reformation tradition but departed from it at two significant points, in its restatement of the relation between church and state and in its insistence that the Word of God is found in Christ alone. It took a stand against the "German Christian" party. Finally, it set forth the one biblical and theological claim that could achieve this, the fact that the proclamation of the Word is to be found in Christ alone, as he is attested to us by Holy Scripture.

Attacks upon the declaration began at once and came from two sides. Lutheran pastors challenged the right of a synod representing more than Lutherans to make a declaration that was binding upon Lutherans, and in so doing they eroded the power of the statement. Simultaneously the church office supported by the Nazis continued, with the help of the dread Gestapo, to take over the administration of church affairs. On June 4, 1936, the chancellor of the Confessing Church sent a lengthy memorandum to Hitler condemning the pagan characteristics of the Nazi state with its racism, concentration camps, secret police methods, destruction of justice, subversion of freedom, and corruption of public morals. It was an act of supreme courage on the part of the writers and of the pastors who read it from their pulpits. Hitler moved rapidly after that to complete his takeover of the church. Karl Koch, who had presided over the Synod of Barmen, was arrested and placed in a concentration camp on July 1, 1937, and remained in Dachau until the war's end. Karl Immer, who had made the arrangements in Barmen for the meeting of the synod, was arrested in August 1937; he quickly became ill and died shortly thereafter. Karl Barth, a Swiss citizen, returned to Switzerland, where he joined the faculty of the University of Basel and remained in that teaching post through his long and distinguished career. Hitler gathered all his power to destroy the church, but with much suffering, some martyrdom, and great devotion, the church, rallying around the Barmen Declaration, remained the one institution of German life that brought a continuing German criticism against Hitler and his Nazi movement.

Two statements sum up the effects of the Barmen Declaration. One is from its author, Karl Barth:

> In 1933 and the years immediately following—at the time that National Socialists "seized power"—there was no struggle of the German universities and schools, of the German legal profession, of German business, of the German theater and German art in general, of the German army, or of the German trade-unions. Many individuals, it is true, went down to an honorable defeat. But in no time at all, those large groups and institutions were subdued and made to conform. On the other hand, from the very first months on there was a German *Church* struggle. Even it was not a total resistance against totalitarian National Socialism. It restricted itself to repelling the encroachment of National Socialism. It confined itself to the Church's Confession, to the Church service, and to

Church order as such. It was only a partial resistance. And for this it has been properly and improperly reproached: properly—in so far as a strong Christian Church, that is, a Church sure of its own cause in the face of National Socialism, should not have remained on the defensive and should not have fought on its own narrow front alone; improperly—in so far as on this admittedly all too narrow front a serious battle was waged, at least in part and not without some success. At any rate, the substance of the Church was rescued and with a better understanding of it than it had had before. If at least as much had been done in other areas as was done at that time in the Church, National Socialism would have had a hard time of it in Germany right from the start. In proportion to its task, the Church has sufficient reason to be ashamed that it did not do more; yet in comparison with those other groups and institutions it has no reason to be ashamed; it accomplished far more than all the rest.[17]

The other statement is from Albert Einstein, a Jew who was the most distinguished scientist of his day, a man who was exiled by Hitler and his policies:

Being a lover of freedom, when the [Nazi] revolution came, I looked to the universities to defend it, knowing that they had always boasted of their devotion to the cause of truth; but no, the universities were immediately silenced. Then I looked to the great editors of the newspapers, whose flaming editorials in days gone by had proclaimed their love of freedom; but they, like the universities, were silenced in a few short weeks. . . .

Only the Church stood squarely across the path of Hitler's campaign for suppressing the truth. I never had any special interest in the Church before, but now I feel a great affection and admiration for it because the Church alone has had the courage and persistence to stand for intellectual and moral freedom. I am forced to confess that what I once despised I now praise unreservedly.[18]

The Confession of 1967

In the years between 1956 and 1967, the Presbyterian Church U.S.A. (from 1958 The United Presbyterian Church U.S.A.) moved in an orderly fashion to restate its faith in a manner consistent with the needs of the last third of the twentieth century.

The movement began quietly enough. In 1956, the Presbytery of Amarillo, Texas, of the PCUSA sent an overture to the General Assembly to ask that the Westminster Shorter Catechism be reworded. The overture was submitted to a special committee for study. The following year the committee reported that it felt the assignment to be unworkable, but recommended that a special committee be named to write a historical introduction to the Shorter Catechism, to revise its biblical references, and to draw up a "brief contemporary statement of faith." This committee was appointed in 1958 with Dr. Edward Dowey of Princeton Theological Seminary as its chairman, and reported its work to the General Assembly meeting in Columbus, Ohio, in 1965.

The report contained three parts: it requested changes in the wording of the ordination questions asked of ministers, elders, and deacons; it recommended not only a new confession of faith but a book of confessions; and it included the first draft of the proposed "Confession of 1967."

Vigorous debate followed, including such questions as whether the document emphasized Jesus' humanity at the expense of his divinity; the lack of mention of the Trinity at key points; the use of the word "normative" to describe the authority of Scripture in the church; and the pointed emphasis on the church's social ministry. The Assembly passed the document, with some amendments, and sent it to the whole church for study. There followed a "mass discussion of theology." Every presbytery gave considerable attention to the document, as did most sessions, and these governing bodies reported suggested changes and amendments to a Committee of Fifteen, who worked to incorporate the best suggestions into the document.

This process took a year. In 1966, when the General Assembly met in Boston, the Committee of Fifteen made its report. Thirty-six amendments were offered from the floor. These were debated at length and all but two rejected. The Assembly gave the document its overwhelming support and recommended it again to the presbyteries for final approval. According to the church's Constitution, two thirds of the presbyteries had to give consent before the confession could be incorporated into the Constitution. Following lengthy debates, more than 90 percent of the presbyteries approved the constitutional changes. At the meeting of the General Assembly in Portland, Oregon, in 1967, the action of the presbyteries and the previous assemblies was affirmed, and the "Confession of 1967," along with new ordination questions and the new Book of Confessions, became part of the Constitution of The United Presbyterian Church in the United States of America.

The Confession of 1967 is built around a single passage of Scripture, 2 Corinthians 5:19, "In Christ God was reconciling the world to himself." The organizing principle around which the confession is built is that of reconciliation, and its three major sections deal with God's work of reconciliation, the ministry of reconciliation, and the fulfillment of reconciliation. The first section is subdivided into three parts: the grace of the Lord Jesus Christ, the love of God, and the communion of the Holy Spirit. The work of ministry is divided into two parts: the mission of the church and the equipment of the church. The fulfillment of reconciliation stands alone.

Chief among the new confessional statements is the statement about Jesus Christ.

In Jesus of Nazareth true humanity was realized once for all. Jesus, a Palestinian Jew, lived among his own people and shared their needs, temptations, joys, and sorrows. He expressed the love of God in word and deed and became a brother to all kinds of sinful people. But his complete obedience led him into conflict with his people. His life and teaching judged their goodness, religious aspirations, and national hopes. Many rejected him and demanded his death. In giving himself freely for them he took upon himself the judgment under which all stand convicted. God raised him from the dead, vindicating him as Messiah and Lord. The victim of sin became victor, and won the victory over sin and death for all. (9.08)[19]

This statement, which for some seems to stress the humanity of Jesus at the expense of his divinity, is balanced by the next paragraph, which speaks of God's work of reconciliation in Jesus Christ.

God's reconciling act in Jesus Christ is a mystery which the Scriptures describe in various ways. It is called the sacrifice of a lamb, a shepherd's life given for his sheep, atonement by a priest; again it is ransom of a slave, payment of debt, vicarious satisfaction of a legal penalty, and victory over the powers of evil. These are expressions of a truth which remains beyond the reach of all theory in the depths of God's love for humanity. They reveal the gravity, cost, and sure achievement of God's reconciling work. (9.09)

This significant statement picks up each major theory of atonement; relates it to Scripture; demonstrates its use of expressions and analogies drawn from the life of the people of God; and uses these as symbols of God's work and our participation in that work. No one theory is given preeminence over the others and the statement neither accepts nor rejects any one theory as determinative for the Christian faith. By interpreting Scripture in this manner, this paragraph is one of the most important in the whole confession both for what it says and for the spirit in which its message is conveyed.

The confession continues: "The risen Christ is the savior for all people. Those joined to him by faith are set right with God and commissioned to serve as his reconciling community. Christ is head of this community . . . , which began with the apostles and continues through all generations. The same Jesus Christ is the judge of all people." (A change from "for" to "of" was made by the Committee of Fifteen and expressed the church's view that judgment encompasses all, while one's response to Christ's saving work was integral to receiving salvation.) "[Christ's] judgment discloses the ultimate seriousness of life and gives promise of God's final victory over the power of sin and death. To receive life from the risen Lord is to have life eternal; to refuse life from him is to choose the death which is separation from God." (The original text had read "to choose death eternal," but this was abandoned on the basis that death is death and without the act of God in resurrection death is final; hence "death eternal" is redundant.) "All who put their trust in Christ face divine judgment without fear, for the judge is their redeemer" (9.10–.11).

The position taken by the Confession of 1967 on the nature and authority of Scripture follows, and this deserves special attention.

It begins with the assertion that the fullness of God's revelation is found in the person of Christ: "The one sufficient revelation of God is Jesus Christ, the Word of God incarnate, to whom the Holy Spirit bears unique and authoritative witness through the Holy Scriptures" (9.27). Noting that "[the Scriptures are to be] received and obeyed as the word of God written," it then moves to its interpretative principle: "The Bible is to be interpreted in the light of its witness to God's work of reconciliation in Christ." The key to understanding Scripture or any portion of it is, what does it tell us of God's reconciling work in Christ? The statement that occasioned the most debate throughout the church follows: "The Scriptures, given under the guidance of the Holy Spirit, are nevertheless the words of men and women, conditioned by the language, thought forms, and literary fashions of the places and times at which they were written" (9.29). The confession continues by stressing the necessity for continuing and careful Bible study: "The church, therefore, has an obligation to approach the Scriptures with literary and historical understanding." There is to be no more uncritical reading of Scripture within the community of Christians. The paragraph ends with the great hope of the church: "As God has spoken his word in diverse cultural situations, the church is confident that he will continue to speak through the Scriptures in a changing world and in every form of human culture" (9.30).

Finally, there is this: "God's word is spoken in his church today where the Scriptures are faithfully preached and attentively read in dependence on the illumination of the Holy Spirit and with readiness to receive their truth and direction" (9.30). The work of the Holy Spirit, according to the confession, is that of fulfilling the work of reconciliation in humankind. The Holy Spirit creates and renews the church as the community in which men and women are reconciled to God and to one another; where they receive forgiveness as they forgive one another; where they enjoy the peace of God as they make peace among themselves; where they are empowered to become representatives of Jesus Christ and his gospel of reconciliation to all people. If God in the Holy Spirit does that work in the church and the world, and if God in the Holy Spirit is to be the illuminator of Scripture, then valid interpretations of Scripture will be found when men and women of the church are engaged in works like these.

The work of the church is clearly delineated in a third section of the Confession of 1967, the Mission of the Church.

The life, death, resurrection, and promised coming of Jesus Christ has set the pattern for the church's mission. . . . His service to men and women commits the church to work for every form of human well-being. His suffering makes the church sensitive to all the sufferings of humanity so that it sees the face of Christ in the faces of people in every kind of need. His crucifixion discloses to the church God's judgment on our inhumanity to each other and the awful consequences of our complicity in injustice. In the power of the risen Christ and the hope of his coming the church sees the promise of God's renewal of

human life in society and of God's victory over all wrong.
(9.32)

The pattern of the ministry of Christ calls for the church to
work in at least four arenas of human life.

One is the arena of inclusivity: "God has created the peoples
of the earth to be one universal family. . . . The church is called
to bring all people to receive and uphold one another as persons in all relationships of life: in employment, housing, education, leisure, marriage, family, church, and the exercise of
political rights. Therefore the church labors for the abolition
of all racial discrimination and ministers to those injured by it"
(9.44).

The second arena is that of peaceful relations between nations: "The search for justice, freedom, and peace requires that
the nations pursue fresh and responsible relations across every
line of conflict, even at risk to national security, to reduce areas
of strife and to broaden international understanding. Reconciliation among nations becomes peculiarly urgent as countries
develop nuclear, chemical, and biological weapons, diverting
their human resources and power from constructive uses and
risking the annihilation of the world" (9.45). God's reconciliation in Christ is the ground for peace, freedom, and justice, and
the church, as well as the individual Christian, is to be God's
agent in fulfilling those purposes.

Poverty is the third problem addressed, and the class structures that support it. "Because Jesus identified himself with the
needy and exploited, the cause of the world's poor is the cause
of his disciples. The church cannot condone poverty, whether
it is the product of unjust social structures, exploitation of the
defenseless, lack of national resources, absence of technological understanding, or rapid expansion of populations. . . . The
church . . . encourages those forces in human society that raise
our hopes for better conditions and provide us with opportu-
nity for a decent living" (9.46).

The fourth arena, sexual relations and family living, was
added as a result of the debates within the church. Speaking

to the existing anarchy and alienation in current sexual relations, the confession proclaims: "Reconciled to God, people have joy in and respect for their own humanity and that of other persons; a man and woman are enabled to marry, to commit themselves to a mutually shared life, and to respond to each other in sensitive and lifelong concern; parents receive the grace to care for children in love and to nurture their individuality" (9.47).

No other official document of any church (the only exceptions are the documents of the Second Vatican Council of the Roman Catholic Church, which were being written at the same time and addressed to the same revolutionary world situation) has so explicitly directed the church to minister to conditions inherent in the world; none gives such clear guidelines for this ministry. The church does so because "God's redeeming work in Jesus Christ embraces the whole of human life: social and cultural, economic and political, scientific and technological, individual and corporate. . . . Already God's reign is present as a ferment in the world, stirring hope . . . and preparing the world to receive its ultimate judgment and redemption. With an urgency born of this hope the church applies itself to present tasks and strives for a better world. . . . In steadfast hope the church looks beyond all partial achievement to the final triumph of God" (9.53–.55).

Since 1967 the Presbyterian Church has set itself to working out this hope in this world in faithfulness and obedience to the God who is continuously revealed to us in Jesus Christ, the church's Lord.

A Brief Statement of Faith

In the early afternoon of Friday, June 10, 1983, two groups of people left the Convention Center in Atlanta, Georgia, by two different doors, and then the two lines merged in the middle of a nearby street. They marched together down the street to the City Hall, where the Reverend Andrew Young, His Honor the mayor of the city of Atlanta and a minister of

the United Church of Christ, addressed them. One of the
groups was made up of commissioners to the General Assembly of the United Presbyterian Church in the United States of
America and their friends, and members of the other group
were commissioners to the General Assembly of the Presbyterian Church in the United States. Each Assembly had met at the
same time in the same building, and they had adjourned their
respective assemblies to become the General Assembly of the
Presbyterian Church (U.S.A.). When the two waves of people
met in the street on that warm spring afternoon, they represented the coming together, after nearly a century and a quarter, of the two mainstream branches of Presbyterianism in the
United States.

These Presbyterians had been divided in the early 1860s by
the Civil War that had split the heart of America into two
pieces. When the War between the States commenced, Presbyterian churches in the confederate states began to pull away
from their northern brothers and sisters. By the fall of that
year, it became clear that there was to be no further commerce
between the Presbyterians of the north and those of the south.
On December 4, 1861, a General Assembly of the Presbyterian churches in the southland met in Augusta, Georgia. Calling themselves "the Presbyterian Church in the Confederate
States," they organized themselves as a new denomination.

This division of 1861 was by no means the first time American Presbyterians had divided from each other. While Presbyterians in the American colonies and later in the United States
of America had conducted distinguished and creative ministries during their whole history, throughout that history divisions and schisms had ripped and torn the fabric of their ecclesiastical body.

1

The first Presbyterian congregations in the colonies were
founded by New England Puritans of Presbyterian conviction
in the 1640s. To these were soon added congregations formed

by immigrants from Scotland and Ireland, who poured into the colonies in the next half-century. By 1706 the first presbytery was founded. Among its seven minister-members were representatives of Scotland, Ireland, and New England. As growth among Presbyterians continued, a synod, composed of nineteen ministers, forty churches, and about three thousand communicants, was organized in 1716.

Schism threatened the new church from its beginning. Many pastors with a Scots or Irish background demanded that all ministers be required to subscribe to the Westminster Confession, together with the Larger and Shorter Catechisms. (This was not, however, the original intention of those who wrote it. Dr. Anthony Tuchney, Professor of Divinity and Vice-Chancellor of Cambridge University at the time, one of the chief authors of the confession and catechisms, said: "In the [Westminster] Assembly I gave my vote with others that the Confession of Faith put out by [our] authority should not be required to be either sworn or subscribed to . . . but [only] as not to be publicly preached or written against.")[20] The New England ministers, plus some from Ireland, opposed this theological restraint. Rupture between the two groups was barely averted in 1729 when a motion before the synod known as the "Adopting Act" was passed. This act required every minister to accept the Westminster standards as determinative for his faith, but not categorically and verbally. It called ministers and candidates to agree that these standards were "in all the essential and necessary articles, good forms of sound words and systems of Christian doctrine." Anyone who did not accept the whole of the standards had to state his scruples concerning the particular part he rejected, and the ordaining body then determined whether that doctrine was essential and necessary to the faith. The Presbyterian Church held together, though just barely, in 1729.

The rise in the colonies of the movement that became known to historians as the First Great Awakening severely tested this fragile compromise. George Whitefield came from England and, along with newly enlivened Methodist preachers, began to preach vigorously about the salvation of souls. Jonathan Edwards of Northampton, Massachusetts, provided a theological base for the message. William and Gilbert Tennent, Presbyterian pastors, insisted that belief in the Bible and orthodox doctrine did not compose a Christian life; a personal experience with God that resulted in high moral standards and religious fervor was essential. "No one ever became a Christian," said the Tennents, "without first passing through the terror of realizing that he was not a Christian." Responding to the Awakening, many ministers and congregations, fearful of the excesses of emotionalism, called for orderliness in the church. In 1741 the Presbyterians split into "Old Side," the traditionalists, and "New Side," the revivalists.

This division, fortunately, was short-lived. In the reconciliation that followed, Old Side insistence on order was preserved, while New Side demands that presbyteries examine ministerial candidates on their experiential acquaintance with religion were met. Coming together again in 1758, the two sides were soon thrust into the cauldron of the Revolutionary War.

Presbyterian churches and church people suffered dreadfully in the war. Over a third of the Presbyterian clergy took some part in the struggle, many taking part in active military service, or as chaplains, or in colonial and state assemblies. Presbyterian churches were desecrated and wantonly destroyed by British troops. Inflation destroyed the whole basis of church finances; First Church, Philadelphia, for one, had to raise pew rents 1,500 percent during the war, and the pastor took no salary for its first six months. When the war finally ended, Presbyterians took steps to organize themselves through a General Assembly, which after years of careful preparation met for the first time in Philadelphia in 1789.

The new General Assembly quickly confronted new problems: how to evangelize the frontier, how to bring the gospel to the whole world, how to meet the growing urbanization of the new United States, what to do about slavery. In the face of these pressing issues, the church eventually split again, in 1837, this time into "Old School" and "New School." In the northern states, Old School and New School parties were about equal in number. Since the New School largely opposed slavery, most of the South was in the Old School camp. For the next thirty-two years, two General Assemblies of Presbyterians met annually.

There was one happy note in this sad dirge of division. In 1858, after twenty years of correspondence and conferences, the Associate Synod and the Associate Reformed Synod, both descended from Scottish Presbyterians who had emigrated to the New World, united to form the United Presbyterian Church of North America.

With the end of the Civil War, the question of reunion again faced the Presbyterians. It was a complicated question. Should Old School and New School reunite, or should the northern Old School and the southern Old School assemblies reunite? In the face of the deep feelings in the nation during the early years of reconstruction, it appeared that only one of these alternatives could be acted upon. A proposal in 1865 by the northern Old School Assembly to invite the southern church to discuss reunion at the same time that reunion was being discussed with the New School Church was voted down. In 1869 in the north, Old School and New School became one church again, but the southern branch of the church, which had been "the Presbyterian Church in the Confederate States," proceeded on its own as "the Presbyterian Church in the United States."

For nearly three quarters of a century, very little action was taken to reunite the split branches of Presbyterianism. But a sense of loss, even of sin, haunted the divided Presbyterians, and in the late 1940s and early 1950s a determined effort was made to unite the Presbyterian Church. A Plan of Union that involved three denominations—Presbyterians north and south and the United Presbyterians—was drawn up. In 1956, when the vote of the presbyteries was counted, the northern church and the United Presbyterian Church of North America favored the union, but the southern church did not support it. Wishing to show the ecumenical world that not all was lost after such effort and prayer, the two denominations that had supported the reunion themselves merged. The year was 1958, exactly one hundred years after the United Presbyterian Church of North America had been formed. Still the dream of reunion persisted. In 1969, both General Assemblies agreed to "seek for a plan for the reunion of the two Churches." Hours, days, years of listening and learning followed. Scores of consultations were held in synods and presbyteries, countless discussions took place in councils, agencies, institutions, and judicatories. Union presbyteries were formed, and they soon contained over fifteen hundred congregations, twenty-three hundred ministers, and four hundred thousand members. Massive cooperative ministries, involving over 150 projects, were engaged in. Plans of reunion were submitted to the denominations for study in 1971, 1974, and 1978. In 1982 a final Plan for Reunion was presented to both General Assemblies. Each found it satisfactory. When it was submitted to the presbyteries, they too upheld it. In June 1983, the General Assemblies of the former churches met for the last time, and the new Presbyterian Church (U.S.A.) was formed.

2

Among the provisions of the Plan for Reunion was a request that "the General Assembly of the reunited Presbyterian Church shall at an early meeting appoint a committee representing diversities of points of view and of groups within the reunited Church to prepare a Brief Statement of the Reformed Faith for possible inclusion in the *Book of Confessions.*" Following the reuniting assembly, Moderator Randolph Taylor complied with this instruction. He appointed a committee of twenty-one persons, chaired by Dr. Jack Stotts, then president of McCormick Seminary, Chicago, and later president of Austin Seminary, Austin, Texas, to prepare the brief statement.

The ecclesiastical situation this committee faced in 1983 was far different from that to which The Confession of 1967 had been addressed only two decades earlier. Reunion of the two denominations was now a fact, and the differences in faith and life between the two former communions had to be reconciled in the new statement. Membership in both denominations had declined dramatically in these two decades, and there was no consensus as to what had precipitated this loss. Liberation and feminist theologies—incarnated in the church by articulate spokespersons for women and minorities—had arisen during these twenty years to challenge the "male–white–Barthian consensus" that had undergirded the Confession of 1967. Conservative groups within both former denominations had gained new status, influence, and friends. Trust in those who directed the work of presbyteries, synods, and especially of the General Assembly, had lowered significantly. The statement of faith to be written by this committee had to confront these and other issues.

Early in their discussion, the committee decided to present a document that could be used widely in worship. This decision limited the size and scope of the Statement. It was to be more like the Nicene and Apostles' creeds in intent and substance than like the Confession of 1967 or the Second Helvetic Confession. The committee met sixteen times for a total of fifty days over five years. Faculty discussions were held at all eleven Presbyterian seminaries and at three corresponding member seminaries. Drafts were shared with the Faith and Order Commission of the National Council of Churches, the National Conference of Catholic Bishops, the Eastern Orthodox Church, and the Evangelical Lutheran Church in America. The World Alliance of Reformed Churches was informed of the committee's work.

A final draft document was sent to the church in December 1987. Fifteen thousand responses came to the committee. The revised draft was presented to the 1989 General Assembly. Further discussion ensued. A second committee was appointed to examine and further revise the Statement. When it was presented again to the 202nd General Assembly, that Assembly approved it and overwhelmingly offered it to the churches for vote. The presbyteries sustained the document, and it was approved in the 203rd General Assembly (1991) for inclusion in the *Book of Confessions.* [21]

3

In an attempt to give renewed theological integrity and ecclesiastical identity to the new denomination, A Brief Statement of Faith is designed for both liturgical and educational use. Consisting of eighty lines and arranged in poetic style, A Brief Statement, like part 1 of the Confession of 1967, takes its shape from the apostolic benediction of 2 Corinthians 13:13. Its opening affirmation echoes the opening question of the Heidelberg Catechism, and this theme is picked up again in the Statement's close. Each line of the Statement echoes the language of Scripture and the Book of Confessions. Throughout, it reflects such catholic doctrines as the Trinity and the full humanity and deity of Jesus. From its Reformed tradition it affirms the basic doctrines of the authority of Scripture, justification by grace through faith, the two sacraments of Baptism and the Lord's Supper, God's sovereignty, election, and God's choice of a covenant people. In response to needs of the current day, it calls Christians to stewardship over God's creation, protests against idolatry, and points out that in God's contemporary world we are ever to seek justice and to live in obedience to the Word of God.

Three themes especially set A Brief Statement of Faith apart from the other creeds and confessions in the Book of Confessions.

1. It gives new prominence to the life and ministry of Jesus Christ:

> Jesus proclaimed the reign of God:
>> preaching good news to the poor
>>> and release to the captives,
>> teaching by word and deed
>>> and blessing the children,
>> healing the sick

> and binding up the brokenhearted,
> eating with outcasts,
> forgiving sinners,
> and calling all to repent and believe the gospel.

> (lines 9–18)

Unlike the Nicene and Apostles' Creeds, which move quickly from Christ's birth to his crucifixion, A Brief Statement brings flesh to the "word made flesh."

2. It affirms the equality in the church of men and women, and it opens all church functions, including ordination, to both women and men:

> In sovereign love God created the world good
> and makes everyone equally in God's image,
> male and female, of every race and people,
> to live as one community.

> (lines 29–32)

> The same Spirit . . . calls women and men to all
> ministries of the church.

> (lines 58, 64)

While this may not be a particularly daring statement to make to Presbyterians who have ordained women to the eldership and diaconate for more than sixty years and to the ministry of Word and Sacrament for more than thirty-five, in its ecumenical context as a statement addressed not only to all Protestants but to Roman Catholics and Orthodox as well, it is revolutionary indeed.

A Brief Statement also includes feminine as well as masculine images of Scripture and God:

> In everlasting love
> the God of Abraham and Sarah chose a covenant
> people
> to bless all families of the earth. . . .
> Loving us still,

God makes us heirs with Christ of the covenant.
Like a mother who will not forsake her nursing child,
like a father who runs to welcome the prodigal home,
God is faithful still.

(lines 41–43, 47–51)

3. As has no creed or confession before it, A Brief Statement calls the church to a new understanding of the church's responsibility for the stewardship of all God's creation.

We rebel against God; we hide from our Creator.
Ignoring God's commandments,
we violate the image of God in others and ourselves,
accept lies as truth,
exploit neighbor and nature,
and threaten death to the planet
entrusted to our care.

(lines 33–38)

Dr. George Kehm, a committee member, wrote of this: God's ideal for our world is that "members of each society participate in bringing about a sustainable use of the earth's resources that is sufficient for the legitimate human needs of its people. . . . 'Entrusted to our care,' " he wrote further, "suggests a renunciation of the popular idea that the Bible authorizes human beings to have 'dominion' over the earth, conquering hostile nature and taking from it whatever human beings want to enhance their survival and to satisfy their desires for delectables and comforts of every sort. . . . (Instead), to serve Christ in our daily tasks means . . . changing our wasteful, polluting life-styles (the way we shop, the food we eat, the clothes we wear, how we decorate and heat our houses, what we do with our garbage, the means of transportation we use). It also includes the decisions we make about the kinds of education and skills we pursue and the kinds of jobs we accept. To claim all of life for Christ includes participation in God's ongoing work to heal and redeem the creation."[22]

4

The searching nature of this last statement reminds us that, for all its strengths, A Brief Statement will need to be supplemented soon by other informed public declarations if Presbyterians, as well as our Christian sisters and brothers, are to receive meaningful direction for ministry in the new century coming. These issues, among others, will need to be addressed.

Because no church or nation, party or system can any longer claim for itself the role of "superpower" and "superparty," we need to confront the pluralisms and ethnicities existent in church, nation, and world.

We need to think through the theological implications of our growing involvement with other religious traditions. Islam, Buddhism, and Hinduism, to name the most prominent, can no longer be considered "quaint vestiges of ancient faiths flowering only in exotic lands," as we may have viewed them a generation ago. Now they may be the living religion of the neighbor who moved next door yesterday, and they are certainly the living faith of millions who inhabit this planet with us today.

We need far better direction than our creeds and confessions have yet provided concerning the way we are to bring the Christian message to those large portions of Western civilization, including a full generation of persons in the United States, who have consciously rejected the Christian faith in favor of their secular lifestyles.

We will need to continue to address the questions surrounding sexuality—marriage and the nurture of children, conception, contraception and abortion, homosexuality, AIDS and other sexually transmitted diseases, abuse of women and children—questions as intimate as our deepest personal identity and as public as the breadth of the human family.

We need to face the questions of human spirituality, the relationship of our spirits to the Spirit of God, and to explore together the spiritual resources of the Reformed tradition, its prayers and worship, preaching and sacraments, moments of meditation, and seasons of retreat and fellowship.

We need to think about life beyond the stars and the impact interplanetary living will have upon our faith and behavior.

We need a far better understanding than we have been given of the way our Christian faith can address the overwhelming urban problems confronting the world in both its southern and northern hemispheres.

We need to relate "the coming new world order" to the coming kingdom of God in Jesus Christ.

Addressing these questions, and the others that our new twenty-first century will surely bring us, will engage the best theological minds and the finest Christian spirits that the church can command in our time.

Conclusion: Order Out of Confusion

Having this number of creeds, confessions, catechisms, and declarations to consider has been confusing to many Presbyterians. How can we deal with so many? Here are four suggestions.

Using The Book of Confessions

1. The first suggestion is to recognize that the *Book of Confessions* provides us with our clearest theological history of Presbyterian doctrine and practice.

"What does it mean to be Presbyterian?" we are frequently asked. Using the *Book of Confessions,* we can confidently reply: Presbyterians are Christians who believe in one God, Father, Son, and Holy Spirit; who recognize their own sin and misery, yet experience God's redemption in Christ, and who are grateful to God for that; who affirm that their faith is in harmony with that of the Christian church through all ages; and who are part of a church that intends to preach the gospel purely, administer the sacraments rightly, and exercise discipline with equity. Presbyterians stand in awe of the sovereignty of God and try to discern the duty they owe to the sovereign God. Presbyterians acknowledge that Jesus Christ is the only Word of God, the sole source of forgiveness of sins, and the only source of the Christian life. They are reconciled to God through Christ, and in response to God's gracious act they set out to reconcile person to person, class to class, nation to nation, and race to race. That, based on the *Book of Confessions,* is what it means to be Presbyterian.

2. A second way to look at the *Book of Confessions* is to think of it as the church's data bank. As such it provides us data to take into account as we consider the issues of our faith.

Take a single example: What is prayer, and how can we pray more effectively? Five of our confessional documents contain sections on prayer, three of which are quite comprehensive.

The Heidelberg Catechism asks, "Why is prayer necessary for Christians?" and it answers, "Because it is the chief part of the gratitude which God requires of us, and because God will give his grace and Holy Spirit only to those who sincerely beseech him in prayer without ceasing, and who thank him for these gifts" (4.116). "What is contained in a prayer which pleases God and is heard by him?" is the next question. Answer: "First, that we sincerely call upon the one true God, who has revealed himself to us in his Word, for all that he has commanded us to ask of him. Then, that we thoroughly acknowledge our need and evil condition so that we may humble ourselves in the presence of his majesty. Third, that we rest assured that, in spite of our unworthiness, he will certainly hear our prayer for the sake of Christ our Lord, as he has promised us in his Word" (4.117). Then the Christian is directed to the Lord's Prayer as containing all things necessary for prayer for body and soul. The last ten questions of the catechism describe the meaning of the Lord's Prayer.

The Westminster Shorter Catechism asks (in a third-person statement rather than the first- and second-person dialogue of the Heidelberg), "What is prayer?" and it answers, "Prayer is an offering up of our desires unto God, for things agreeable to his will, in the name of Christ, with confession of our sins, and thankful acknowledgment of his mercies" (7.098). This catechism, too, concludes its section on prayer, in the last nine questions, by presenting its understanding of the Lord's Prayer.

The Confession of 1967 places its explanation of prayer in a longer section entitled "The Equipment of the Church," and it includes prayer with preaching and teaching, Baptism and the Lord's Supper, as tools the church employs to equip itself for its reconciling mission. "The church responds to the message of reconciliation in praise and prayer. In that response it commits itself afresh to its mission, experiences a deepening of faith and obedience, and bears open testimony to the gospel. Adoration of God is acknowledgment of the Creator by the creation. Confession of sin is admission of our guilt before God and of our need for his forgiveness. Thanksgiving is rejoicing in God's goodness to all and in giving for the needs of others. Petitions and intercessions are addressed to God for the continuation of his goodness, the healing of our ills, and our deliverance from every form of oppression. The arts, especially music and architecture, contribute to the praise and prayer of a Christian congregation when they help us look beyond ourselves to God and to the world which is the object of his love" (9.50).

Note that each document sets prayer in the context of its own theological framework. The Heidelberg Catechism sees prayer as expressing God's goodness, our sin, and God's redemption. The Westminster Confession sees it as an expression of God's sovereignty over us and our duty to God. The Confession of 1967 relates prayer to the church's mission of reconciliation. Two documents point to the Lord's Prayer as our model for prayer. No distinction is made between public and private prayer; the Christian who prays in private also joins in the same spirit with the public prayers of the congregation. The scope of prayer to be offered includes adoration, thanksgiving, confession, petition, intercession, and dedication. Finally, prayer is offered in the name, spirit, and, often, in the very words, of Jesus Christ himself.

By providing us such an in-depth consideration of the subject of prayer, the *Book of Confessions* acts as the church's data bank on this issue. It does so for numerous other questions of Christian faith and life. As long as we have our *Book of Confessions,* we as Presbyterians are never left without resources for understanding the Christian faith.

3. We can also use the *Book of Confessions* in widely varied areas of the church's life.

Portions can be used in worship. The Apostles' Creed and the Nicene Creed have always been employed as statements of faith, but their use can be supplemented by sections of the Confession of 1967 and the affirmation found in Answer 1 of the Heidelberg Catechism. The first answer in the Shorter Catechism can be part of a confession of sins, and statements on the meaning of the Lord's Supper are valuable as the basis for prayers during that service. Use of the *Book of Confessions* in liturgy is limited only by the imaginations and perceptions of those who plan and preside at worship.

It can be used in preaching, as it has been for centuries. Ministers can interpret biblical passages in the light of the interpretation offered in the confessions. Themes for preaching can be drawn from the confessions in those congregations that do not follow the lectionary. Whole sections, such as those in the Heidelberg Catechism, can be used on consecutive Sundays or for special seasons or series of sermons.

In ministries of Christian education, the confessions can be a resource to enable children, youth, and adults to understand what it means to be a Christian within the Reformed tradition. the *Book of Confessions* can be used in commissioning classes to help students understand the sacraments and the theology of the church. Pastors can find guidance in the theology and language of the confessions for what they say and do in ministering to persons. The confessions can set guidelines for use in evangelism, mission, administration, church order and discipline. Above all, they can be rallying points in times of danger and persecution. Uses will be determined as sessions and congregations become increasingly familiar with the *Book of Confessions*.

4. Finally, we need to see the *Book of Confessions* in the light of the total theological position of the Presbyterian Church.

We must, of course, realize that the confessions are always subservient to Scripture. Scripture, with its witness to Christ, is the standard for all faith and practice for Presbyterians.

Individual confessions are statements of what Scripture has led the church to believe and do in the specific situation out of which they grew and to which they are addressed. As stated in the report on "The Confessional Nature of the Church," in a recommendation adopted by the 198th General Assembly (1986) of the Presbyterian Church (U.S.A.):

> The confessions of the Book of Confessions are standards, in response to the historical context of the time, which are subordinate to Scripture; they are subject to criticism in light of the Word of God in Jesus Christ as witnessed in the Scriptures of the Old and New Testaments and may be revised by the church following duly prescribed procedures. (29.206)[23]

As Presbyterians we live our lives in obedience to Jesus Christ—this is always first and fundamental—under the authority of Scripture, without which we cannot know the Christ; and only after that we are to be guided and instructed by our confessions.

The report also points out that when there are differences between confessions, initial priority should be given to contemporary confessions. Yet the report hastens to add that "this is only initial preference because further reflection may reveal that at some points the church in earlier times was more able and willing to be guided by the Spirit than the contemporary church [is]" (29.187).

Where there are conflicts in understanding what it is necessary and essential to believe and say about some issue, it is the ascending sequence of governing bodies that make final decisions. Resolving conflicts that may grow out of either study or application of the confessions takes us to the heart of Presbyterian polity, with its carefully worked out procedures for facing issues decently and in order, in which the guidance and instruction of the *Book of Confessions* is a single and necessary part.

The Constitution of the Presbyterian Church (U.S.A.) also makes it clear that no list of "essential tenets" will ever be compiled. Such a list would reduce the content of the confessions to a few selected basic doctrines and would undercut the richness and diversity that a Book of Confessions is designed to produce. It would also undermine the power of the Holy Spirit to lead the church to new understandings that might emerge from prayerfully studying these historic documents, a power that no checklist of articles of faith, however precisely worded, can ever preempt for itself. "Faith in the living God present and at work in the risen Christ through the Holy Spirit means always to be open to hear a new and fresh word from the Lord" (29.151).

Each minister, elder, and deacon, therefore, needs to study the *Book of Confessions* so that she or he may be instructed, led, and continually guided by these creeds and confessions. Free from the need to give unqualified assent to everything the confessions state and from legalistic interpretations of these documents, each officer commits himself or herself to inquire into the book to see what light God through the Holy Spirit of Christ is casting upon the baffling issues and perplexing situations that are confronting the church in our day.

A Plan for Study

The purpose of this book is to help you become familiar with the *Book of Confessions.* There are a number of ways individuals and groups may approach such a study.

Set a personal schedule for study. Do you want to read one document a month? Under such a plan anyone could finish the book within a year. Reading one confession a quarter would mean that during the three-year term of office every officer would have read the entire *Book of Confessions.* Read the confession with the description of it given in this study. Whatever the schedule, each officer should plan his or her own program for becoming acquainted with the book; each has pledged at ordination to do so.

A second way to study the *Book of Confessions* is to do so as a group. A new class of officers may read and study together using either the five-session course or the nine-session course suggested in Appendix A. A weekend retreat can be scheduled to follow one or the other of the courses. A group may determine that it will consider one confession at a time as part of a continuing study program at board meetings.

Presbyteries may also offer studies. Some have weekend programs that include a number of study possibilities and a course on the confessions can become part of this. Pre-presbytery assemblies can be used to offer studies of the confessions. Use the confessions as part of worship services and celebrations. We can look forward to the sixtieth anniversary of the Barmen Declaration in 1994 and the thirtieth anniversary of the Confession of 1967 in 1997. In 1993 we can celebrate the three hundred and fiftieth anniversary of the opening of the Westminster Assembly and in 1997 the writing of the Westminster Confession and the Larger and Shorter Catechisms. The four hundred and fiftieth anniversaries of the Scots Confession, the Heidelberg Catechism, and the Second Helvetic Confession fall, respectively, in the years 2010, 2013, and 2016. These years will provide opportunities for presbyteries, as well as for congregations, to celebrate the theological heritage that has shaped our church and our personal lives.

This introduction to the *Book of Confessions* is only the beginning of our consideration of this book. Whatever your present familiarity with it, it is more important to be reading it than to have read it, more significant to be studying it than to have studied it. The report to the General Assembly summarizes the matter this way: "The Book of Confessions as a whole enriches our understanding of what it means to be a Reformed Christian, helps us escape the provincialism to which we have been prone, and expresses our intention to join the worldwide family of Reformed churches that is far bigger and more inclusive than our particular denomination" (29.168).

Appendixes

The appendixes that follow include: (A) a guide for a five-session course of study, with suggestions for expanding the study to ten sessions; and (B) an index, in tabular form, of theological subjects found in the *Book of Confessions*.

The study guide can be adapted for use in a congregation or for a presbytery event. Because the confessions are documents that cannot be studied casually, the study guide reflects the depth and seriousness of the original documents. If the guide is to be used effectively, leaders will need to prepare themselves for the task by reading the confession to be discussed and the appropriate chapter in *We Believe* that discusses it. Additional information from other books on the confessions or other church histories would also be helpful. The study guide focuses on the topics that this writer considers most important; in preparation for particular classes each leader will need to identify which of these issues is most important to the congregation or presbytery in which the study is conducted and prepare accordingly.

The index or compendium of theological subjects will help individuals and classes trace the growth and development of the theological concepts expressed in the confessions and is a unique tool for giving guidance in doing so.

Appendix A
Study Guide for the Creeds and Confessions

Five Sessions

Session 1: *The Creeds of the Early Church*

Locate both Rome and Constantinople (Istanbul) on a map. Ask the group to recite both creeds, the Apostles' and the Nicene.

The Apostles' Creed
Consider Marcion and the impact of his attack on the Christian faith. How do we use the Old Testament today?

Discuss the theological issues that are reflected in the creed: forgiveness of sins; the universality of the church; purity in the moral life.

Discuss the use of the creed in the church today: in worship and in baptism.

The Nicene Creed
How do we view Jesus Christ, as Arius did or as Athanasius did?

What does the creed tell us about our current understanding of God as Father? God as Son? God as Holy Spirit?

How do you explain "One God in Three Persons" to a non-Christian?

Close the session with worship, thanking God for the creeds, for the men and women who helped to write them, for the insights into the Christian faith that they give us, and for our continued use of them in our churches.

Session 2: *Reformation Documents* (The Scots Confession, the Heidelberg Catechism, and the Second Helvetic Confession)

Using a map, locate Wittenberg, Germany; Geneva, Switzerland (the two centers of the Reformation); Heidelberg, Germany; and St. Andrews and Edinburgh in Scotland. What differences can you identify in the way the Reformation proceeded in each country?

From the information in chapter 2 of this book about the writers of these documents—John Knox, Caspar Olevianus, Zacharias Ursinus, and Heinrich Bullinger—how have the patterns of ministry these men established influenced our understanding of ministry today?

Outline the major beliefs of each of these documents (see chart in the introduction). How do they influence our beliefs today?

The Reformation writers called Jesus "The Anointed One: Prophet, Priest, and King." (See especially 4.031.) What do these terms mean to us today? What other meaningful titles do you give Christ today?

Close with worship built around the faith expressed in the opening statement of the Heidelberg Catechism.

Session 3: *The Westminster Documents*

Begin by considering the changes that had taken place in the world between the 1560s, when the later Reformation creeds were written, and the 1640s, when the Westminster Confession was drawn up. Include such matters as the colonization of the Americas and the opening of lands in the East, the defeat of the Spanish Armada and the way it affected all of Europe, the change from the Tudors to the Stuarts in England, the wars between Protestants and Catholics in Europe, the development of the new sciences, and the growing secularization of culture.

What changes took place in the churches in these eighty years in response to those conditions?

The major theological position of the Westminster Confession is that God is sovereign and that men and women owe a duty to the Sovereign God. How has that position affected your life as a Presbyterian? What alternate theological position, if any, do you hold today?

The Westminster Confession states that "the unlearned, in a due use of the ordinary means, may attain unto a sufficient understanding of [Scripture]" (6.007). The Confession of 1967 says: "The church . . . has an obligation to approach the Scriptures with literary and historical understanding" (9.29). How do you reconcile these two statements?

The study book makes a point of the relationship between religious points of view and political positions: the Anglicans supported the King against Parliament, the Presbyterians affirmed representative government in both church and state, the Independents stood for local control of both church and government. Explore some of the ways that religion affects our political thinking today, and vice versa.

What does this confession tell us about the relation between church and state? (See especially 6.127–.130.) Do you agree or disagree with this statement? Why?

What factors beyond those included in the Westminster Confession do we need to take into account as our church writes its new confession of faith today?

Build the closing worship service around the section on prayer in the Westminster Shorter Catechism (7.098).

Session 4: *Twentieth-Century Creeds (The Barmen Declaration, the Confession of 1967, and the Brief Statement of Faith)*

Discuss the conditions in Germany and in the United States that occasioned the writing of each document.

The Barmen Declaration declares: "Jesus Christ, as he is attested for us in Holy Scripture, is the one Word of God which we have to hear and which we have to trust and obey in life and in death" (8.11). How does this fit with your understanding of the Bible as the Word of God?

The Barmen Declaration points out that "Jesus Christ is God's assurance of forgiveness of all our sins" (8.14) and indicates that because forgiveness is found in no other, it is from Christ's offer of forgiveness that the church has its authority today. Do we still find forgiveness in and through Christ's church today? Do we still find it *only* in and through the church? Do we find forgiveness at all? Do we consider Christ's offer of forgiveness for sin as important in our lives as it is said to be in this statement in the Barmen Declaration?

The Barmen Declaration insists we belong wholly to Christ and not to other lords, for justification and sanctification is only in Christ (see 8.14–.15). Is our behavior as Christians today basically determined by our faith in Christ or do we build our standards of conduct on the basis of other beliefs—political, cultural, personal? Where do you find evidence for your position?

The Confession of 1967 describes the church's mission as growing out of the ministry of Jesus Christ (9.32). How does the ministry of your congregation fit this pattern?

The Confession of 1967 speaks of the necessity for the church to be a reconciling agent in society. How is this expressed in your congregation's ministry: in racial affairs, in national struggles, in situations of class differences, within families?

The Confession of 1967 describes our "new life in Christ" (9.21–.26). Compare this description to your own personal Christian life. How do you fit this pattern? Is the pattern adequate to describe our life in Christ? How might you suggest changes in the pattern?

A Brief Statement of Faith talks about the equality in the church of women and men. Is this true in our church? It also talks of the possibility that our unfaithfulness to God can destroy our planet. Do you think this is really possible?

Use the description of "Praise and Prayer" (9.50) as the basis for closing worship.

Session 5: *Order Out of Confusion*

Having so many creeds and confessions may cause some confusion in the church and in our personal lives; there is no "one place to turn" to find "the Presbyterian answer" to an issue or to questions of faith. Do you consider this to be good or bad? Why?

Turning to Appendix B, take one theological concept and trace its development from document to document. Did you find any contradictions in the statements? If so, how do you make choices between them? How do you reconcile them?

Discuss further some of the following ideas, expressed in the last chapter of the book. (Give as much time as needed to each discussion; fifteen minutes for each may not be enough to explore the issue!):

The *Book of Confessions* enriches our faith.

A principle for interpreting the *Book of Confessions* is that the later documents take precedence over the earlier ones.

The *Book of Confessions* needs to be corrected by Scripture and is always subordinate to it. How does this work out in practice?

Each officer of the church needs to be "guided and informed" by the *Book of Confessions*.

How can you make more use of the *Book of Confessions* in your church—In worship? In Christian Education? In session discussions?

Plan your closing worship around the idea taken from the

report to the 198th General Assembly (1986) on "The Confessional Nature of the Church" (29.168): "The Book of Confessions as a whole enriches our understanding of what it means to be Reformed Christians, helps us escape the provincialism to which we have been prone, and expresses our intention to join the worldwide family of Reformed churches that is far bigger and more inclusive than our particular denomination."

Ten Sessions

The resources are easily expanded for a ten-session course, devoting one session to each text. The third and fifth sessions of the shorter course are used unchanged for sessions 6 and 9.

Session 1: *The Apostles' Creed*

Have the group recite the creed together.

What were some of the conditions in the church that caused the creed to be written? Are there any situations analogous to this today that might need to be addressed in writing a new confession for our denomination?

Are there words and phrases in the creed that need to be interpreted for our time? What are they? Where do we turn for help in interpreting them?

Consider Marcion and the impact of his attack on the Christian faith. How do we use the Old Testament today? Discuss the following theological issues, reflected in the creed: forgiveness of sins; the universality of the church; purity in the moral life. Consider the use of the creed in the church today: in worship and in baptism.

What are other places where the creed might be used in your congregation's life? Do you feel that we use it enough? What are some problems encountered in using the creed? What might happen if you never used it?

Let your closing worship for this session reflect your use of the creed and your new understanding of it.

Session 2: *The Nicene Creed*

Begin by reciting the Nicene Creed.

On a map locate both Rome (where the Apostles' Creed was first composed) and Constantinople (Istanbul). How much difference was there in the practice of religion in the West and in the East? What conditions in the Roman empire contributed to this? To what degree were there differences in culture between Rome and Constantinople? Why were there two centers of the empire?

In writing a new creed for the church, what would you include in it that is not found in the Nicene Creed?

How do we view Jesus Christ, as Arius did or as Athanasius did?

What does the creed tell us about our current understanding of God as Father? God as Son? God as Holy Spirit?

How do you explain "One God in Three Persons" to a non-Christian?

Would you consider this creed primarily a document of belief or primarily a vehicle for praise and worship? Why?

Close with worship, thanking God for the creeds we have studied to date, for the men and women who helped write them, for the insights into the Christian faith that they give us, and for our continued use of them in our churches.

Session 3: *The Scots Confession*

Using a map, locate Wittenberg, Germany; Geneva, Switzerland (the two centers of the Reformation); St. Andrews and Edinburgh in Scotland. What differences can you identify in the way the Reformation proceeded in each country?

Recall as much information as you can about John Knox, one of the writers of this confession. How does his situation in Scotland compare or contrast with our situation today in the United States?

Outline the confession, indicating its various themes. How do you feel about the anti-Catholic feeling of this document?

The confession states: "The notes of the true Kirk [are]: the true preaching of the Word of God; . . . the right administration of the sacraments; . . . and . . . ecclesiastical discipline uprightly ministered" (3.18). Are these sufficient to describe the ministry of the church today?

The *Book of Order* of the Presbyterian Church (U.S.A.) extends these into "The Six Great Ends of the Church" (G-1.0200). Compare and contrast these. What other goals would you add to guide the church in ministry today?

Discuss the implications of Section XXIV (3.24), "The Civil Magistrate," for our understanding of church and state today.

Focus the closing worship upon some of the psalm paraphrases in our current hymnals and indicate which they are, where they come from, why they were used, and what they mean to us.

Session 4: *The Heidelberg Catechism*

Review the conditions under which this catechism was written. Call attention to the outline of the catechism: human misery, God's grace, our gratitude. How could it be said that this is a primary theological framework for our thinking today?

Note the place given to the law in this catechism: to keep the commandments is part of our gratitude to God. Do we view "keeping the commandments" in this kind of context? List some examples.

This catechism called Jesus "the Anointed One: Prophet, Priest, and King" (see especially 4.031). What do these terms mean to us today? What other meaningful titles do you give Christ today?

What insights from this confession would you incorporate in a confession written in our time?

Close with worship built around the faith expressed in the opening statement of the Heidelberg Catechism.

Session 5: *The Second Helvetic Confession*

From the material in chapter 2 of this book, recall the setting in Zurich and Heidelberg from which the Second Helvetic Confession comes. Review the issues of the day that influenced the writing of the confession.

Consider the model of ministry that Bullinger presented; it is further developed in 5.142, .144, .146–.147, .153, .155–.165. Since it is the basic model developed in the Reformation, is it still an adequate model for conducting ministry today? How do we agree with it and how do we differ from it?

Bullinger has a distinct doctrine of interpreting Scripture (see 5.001, .010–.013). What does it have to say to the church today?

Bullinger's doctrine of predestination differed somewhat from Calvin's and has proved very attractive to the church (see 5.052–.061). What direction does it give to us today as we think through this difficult issue?

Bullinger also has a full discussion of the sacraments (see 5.169, .172–.173, 5.178–.180). What emphases in these sections need to be held before the church today? Why?

To complete the session, compose a short service of worship that will reflect the temperate and thoughtful spirit of Bullinger.

Session 6: *The Westminster Documents*

Use the third session of the shorter course (page 108).

Session 7: *The Barmen Declaration*

Discuss the conditions in Germany that occasioned the writing of this document.

The Barmen Declaration states: "Jesus Christ, as he is attested for us in Holy Scripture, is the one Word of God which we have to hear and which we have to trust and obey in life and in death" (8.11). How does this fit with an understanding of the Bible as the Word of God?

The Barmen Declaration points out that "Jesus Christ is God's assurance of the forgiveness of all our sins" (8.14) and indicates that because forgiveness is found in no other, it is from Christ's offer of forgiveness that the church receives its authority today. Do we still find forgiveness in and through Christ's church today? Do we still find it only in and through the church? Do we find forgiveness at all? Do we consider Christ's offer of forgiveness for sin to be as important in our lives as it is said to be in the Barmen Declaration?

The Barmen Declaration insists we belong wholly to Christ and not to other lords, for justification and sanctification is only in Christ (see 8.14–.15). Is our behavior as Christians today basically determined by our faith in Christ or do we build our standards of conduct on the basis of other beliefs—political, cultural, personal? List some examples.

Because of the situation in which the Synod of Barmen found itself (that is, confronted with the dictates of Adolf Hitler), its position on the place of government in God's divine economy is different from that of other documents (see 8.22–.24). What does this section have to say to people in our country today?

Develop the worship service that concludes this session around the Scripture found in the Barmen Declaration: read each passage and compose a prayer that expresses the major idea contained in the passage chosen by Karl Barth and his fellow writers.

Session 8: *The Confession of 1967*

This confession, unlike most of the others, did not come from a period of overt and recognized crisis in the church. Reconstruct the situation in church and nation that called forth this confession. Include such matters as the Vietnam War, the racial tensions, the student revolts, the growing threat of nuclear weapons, and the church's response to these.

The Confession of 1967 describes the church's mission as growing out of the ministry of Jesus Christ (9.32). How does the ministry of your congregation fit this pattern?

The confession speaks of the necessity of the church being a reconciling agent in society. How do you express that in your congregation's ministry: in racial affairs, in national struggles, in situations of class differences, within families?

The confession describes our "new life in Christ" (9.21–.26). Compare this description to your own personal Christian life. How do you fit this pattern? Is the pattern adequate to describe our life in Christ? How might you suggest changes in the pattern?

Choose some section of the confession that is especially meaningful to you and discuss it with members of the class: what is it and why is it meaningful to you?

Use the description of "Praise and Prayer" in 9.50 as the basis for closing worship.

Session 9: *A Brief Statement of Faith*

Read together, as an act of worship, the whole Brief Statement.

If possible, view the twelve-minute videotape on the Brief Statement of Faith prepared by the former Theology and Worship Ministry Unit. It can be secured from presbytery Resource Centers.

Consider the question: What is God doing in the world today, through the second Person of the Trinity (Jesus Christ)? through the first person (the God of Abraham and Sarah)? through the third Person (God as Spirit)?

Ask: Since God is doing all this, what ought we be doing in response to God's work?

Consider some of the scriptural and confessional resources that the committee used in writing the Brief Statement: 2 Corinthians 13:13; Luke 4; Isaiah 61; Acts 2:32; Genesis 3:8;

Ephesians 2:8; Romans 5; and Matthew 28:16–20 are appropriate, as are Question 1 of the Heidelberg Catechism and Thesis One of the Barmen Declaration.

To close the session, worshipfully recite A Brief Statement once more.

Session 10: *Order Out of Confusion*

Use the fifth session of the shorter course (page 111).

Appendix B
Index to the Book of Confessions

Topic	Nicene, Apostles' Creeds	Scots Confession	Heidelberg Catechism	Second Helvetic Confession
Nature of God		3.01		5.015
Creator God	1.1; 2.1		4.026	5.032
Providence			4.027–.028	5.029–.031
Trinity		3.01	4.025	5.015–.019
Evil				5.041,.044
Human Nature		3.02–.03	4.006	5.034,.045
Sin			4.005–.008	5.036–.039
Covenant		3.04–.05		
Jesus Christ	1.2; 2.2	3.06–.08	4.029–.036	5.062–.079
Cross, Atonement	1.2; 2.2	3.09	4.037–.044	5.071,.076
Resurrection	1.2; 2.2	3.10	4.045,.057	5.073,.076
Election		3.08	4.052,.054	5.052–.061
Holy Spirit	1.3; 2.3	3.12	4.053	5.018
Justification			4.060	5.106–.111
Faith			4.061–.064	5.112–.123
Repentance			4.088–.090	5.093–.094
Scripture		3.19		5.001–.014
Prayer			4.116–.129	5.218–.222
Sacraments		3.21–.23	4.065–.068	5.169–.184
Baptism			4.069–.074	5.185–.192
Lord's Supper			4.075–.085	5.193–.210
Christian Life		3.12–.14	4.001–.002 4.086–.115	5.112–.123
Worship			4.096–.098 4.103	5.020–.028 5.211–.231, .240–.242
Church	1.3; 2.3	3.05,.16,.18	4.054	5.124–.141
Mission				
Church and Civil Government		3.24		5.252–.258
Future		3.17,.25	4.057–.058	

Westminster Confession	Westminster Shorter Catechism	Westminster Larger Catechism	Barmen Declaration	Confession of 1967	A Brief Statement of Faith
6.011–.012	7.004	7.117			II. 5–6, 28–32, 40–71, 79–80
6.022–.023	7.009	7.125		9.16	II. 29–32
6.014–.015 6.024–.030	7.008–.011,.- 012	7.128–.130			II. 40–51
6.013	7.006	7.119–.121			II. 2–5, 7–8, 27–28, 52–53, 72–73, 80
6.027					II. 33–39
6.023	7.010	7.127		9.17	II. 8, 29–40, 55–57
6.031–.036	7.013–.019	7.131–.139		9.12–.14	II. 33–39, 65, 69–71
6.037–.042	7.020	7.140–.146		9.18–.19	II. 40–51
6.043–.050	7.021–.026	7.146–.155	8.10–.15	9.08–.11	II. 7–28
6.047	7.027	7.156–.160			II. 19–22
	7.028	7.161–.162			II. 23–26
6.016–.021 (cf.6.055–.058)	7.020	7.123			II. 41–51
6.051–.054	7.029	7.168		9.20	II. 52–79
6.068–.073	7.033	7.180–.181,.187			II. 54
6.078–.080		7.182–.183			II. 5, 7, 27, 52, 77–79
6.081–.086	7.087	7.186			II. 33–40
6.001–.010	7.002–.003 7.088–.090	7.113–.115	8.11–.12	9.27–.30,.49	II. 58–61
6.114,.115, .117	7.098–.107	7.288–.306		9.50	II. 66–67, 76
6.149–.153	7.091–.093	7.271–.274			II. 62–63
6.154–.160	7.094–.095	7.275–.277		9.51	II. 62
6.161–.168	7.096–.097	7.278–.285		9.52	II. 63
6.075–.077 6.087–.107 6.112–.119	7.030–.036 7.039–.081 7.001	7.175–.193 7.201–.258 7.111	8.13–.15 9.48–.52	9.21 .26	II. 54–79
(cf.6.191– .193)	7.045–.062	7.213–.231			II. 54–64, 80
6.140–.145		7.171–.175	8.16–.21		II. 54–76
6.187–.190			8.25–.27	9.31–.47	II. 54–76
6.127–.130			8.22–.24	9.17,.25	II. 69–71
6.180–.182	7.037–.038	7.192–.200		9.11,.26 9.53–.56	II. 72–80

Developed by M. McCoy Franklin, pastor of First Presbyterian Church, Auburn, Alabama.

Notes

1. *The Constitution of the Presbyterian Church (U.S.A.)*, Part I, *Book of Confessions* (New York: Office of the General Assembly, 1983).

2. *Minutes of the 198th General Assembly of the Presbyterian Church (U.S.A.) 1986*, part I, *Journal*; report of the Advisory Council on Discipleship and Worship, on "The Confessional Nature of the Church," para. 29.113.

3. Ibid., 29.122.

4. My translation.

5. Robert Lowry Calhoun, *Lectures on the History of Christian Doctrine* (privately published; New Haven: Yale Divinity School, 1948), vol. 1, p. 142.

6. Ibid., vol. 1, p. 147.

7. Translation of the Nicene Creed from *Prayers We Have in Common* (Philadelphia: Fortress Press, 1975), copyright © 1970, 1971, and 1975 by International Consultation on English Texts. This translation is used, with slight changes for inclusive language, in *The Service for the Lord's Day: The Worship of God*, Supplemental Liturgical Resource 1 (Philadelphia: Westminster Press, 1984).

8. A paraphrase of the first question and answer of the Heidelberg Catechism, arranged to be used liturgically. The translation used in the *Book of Confessions* may be similarly arranged.

9. John T. McNeill, *The History and Character of Calvinism* (New York: Oxford University Press, 1954), p. 324.

10. Philip Schaff, *The Creeds of Christendom* (Grand Rapids: Baker Book House, 1977), vol. 1, p. 729. Reprinted from edition by Harper & Brothers, New York, 1877.

11. Arthur C. Cochrane, *The Church's Confession Under Hitler* (Philadelphia: Westminster Press, 1962), pp. 222–223.

12. Ibid., p. 109.
13. Ibid., p. 236.
14. Ibid., pp. 255–256.
15. Ibid., pp. 260–261.
16. Ibid., p. 262.
17. Ibid., pp. 40–41.
18. Ibid., p. 40.
19. Quotations from the Confession of 1967 have been slightly altered to employ inclusive language.
20. Quoted in Schaff, *The Creeds of Christendom,* vol. 1, p. 760.
21. Jack A. Rogers, *Presbyterian Creeds: Supplement on A Brief Statement of Faith* (Louisville, Ky.: Westminster/John Knox Press, 1991), gives an excellent and detailed study of the meeting-by-meeting working of both committees.
22. *To Confess the Faith Today,* ed. Jack Stotts, and Jane Dempsey Douglass (Louisville, Ky.: Westminster/John Knox Press, 1990), pp. 89–91.
23. This and subsequent references are to the Report of the Advisory Council on Discipleship and Worship to the 198th General Assembly (1986). See note 2 above.